Building a High Performance Team with DISC Profiling

Tools for rapid growth companies

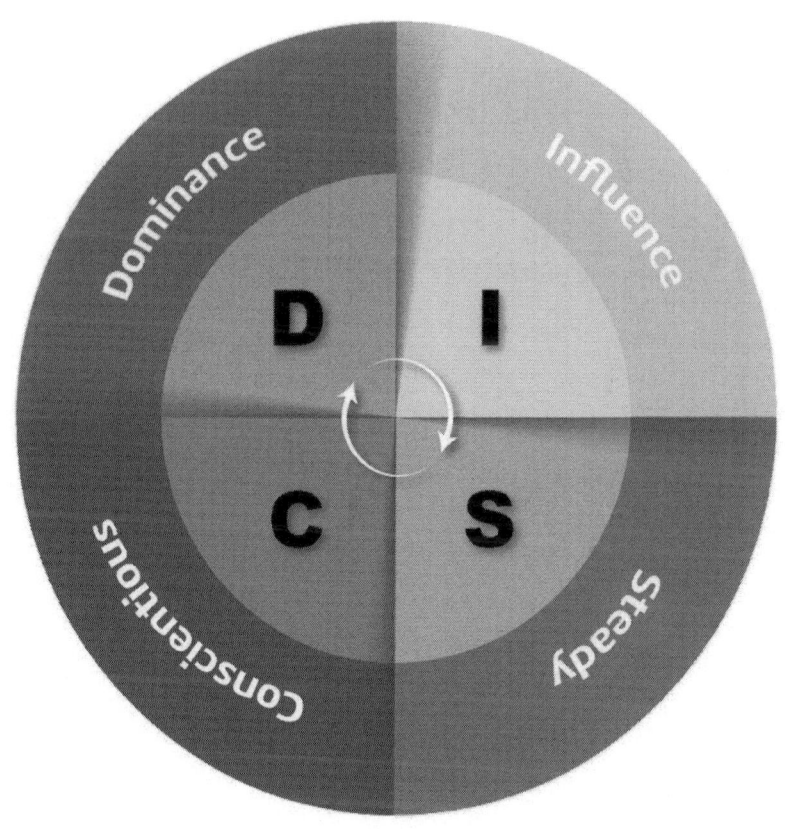

Copyright © Craig Robinson 2016

You can contact the author at www.craigdrobinson.com
ISBN: 978-1539469674
Cover Design: Nicola Swankie
Interior Design: DFSI Pty Ltd
Publisher: CDR Publishers
Editor: Carrie Bean

1. Business 2. People Management 3. Entrepreneurship
4. Team work

Table of Contents

Introduction

It's not always as easy to deal with employees as you might wish. Some require more control while others prefer to be left to work alone. Others will be more outgoing while some can be a little reserved.

Some employees may also focus on tasks. Others are patient and willing to take a while. There are even those who are extremely precise and want to be perfect.

Creating a team is even harder. Employees who behave and think differently can clash with one another.

However, that does not mean you cannot take control of the situation. You can use the DISC test to decide which employees are suited to certain tasks.

Specifically, the DISC test looks into the behaviours of individual employees. It helps you determine who's more outgoing, who is goal-oriented and whether or not certain people are good with change.

This isn't a personality-based test. It's a test that reviews behaviours. More importantly, it takes a look at how people interpret their environments.

This book is about the DISC test, how to administer it and the results that will come from it. It gives you an insight into how your employees or potential hires will respond to their environments. Amazingly, it only takes a few minutes to perform the test. You can even do this online if required.

There are also a number of different behavioural styles that you'll find through a DISC test. Each of these types are profiled alongside their key features and weaknesses.

This guide will also show you how to deal with issues that come with the test. Details on how to complete the test properly are included.

It's essential to run your current or prospective employees through the DISC test. It's all about knowing how your employees will behave and respond to tasks.

You should also be aware that some of your competitors might be using the DISC test. The actions you take after the test is given can influence your workplace.

Chapter 1 – Understanding the Need for the DISC Process

How big is your organisation? _team_ The odds are you've got lots of tasks to work with but not enough time or energy for you to do it on your own. That's when the assistance of your employees and other group members can come in handy.

You can do anything you want to get people into a group. You can hire as many people as you want and give them a variety of tasks. However, it will not mean a thing if you don't understand how your team operates.

Having a strong team in the workplace makes a big difference. Proficient teams complete more tasks more efficiently and won't argue with one another.

Teamwork is critical to your success; no single person should be held higher than anyone else. However, the process of assembling a team is no easy task.

Everyone has their own attitudes towards specific tasks. Employees will approach and finish their projects in various ways and will develop conflicts with others if they don't agree.

Fortunately, it's not too hard to figure out how people behave. You can use the DISC test to figure out which employees go well with each other.

MISL

DISC Model of Behavior

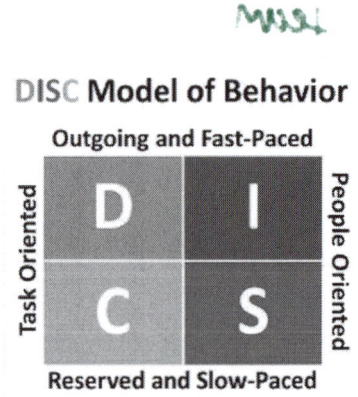

The DISC process is a simple solution devoted to helping you find which people have the best traits in your business climate. This assessment tool has been around for decades to identify various characteristics like a person's dominance, how well someone can comply with ideas and so forth.

The DISC test is designed to analyse these characteristics in anyone. It illustrates how well people behave in certain environments, going well beyond just personality. It especially focuses on how people act in team-based situations or in stressful circumstances. It reviews how well employees perceive power.

This is not necessarily designed to predict exactly how people will act in certain situations. Rather, it helps you to understand what people are likely to do. It helps people learn more about each other.

This process is important; there are many reasons why this process is crucial when trying to start a project.

It Helps to Organise Groups

Your groups must always be organised the right way. Still, it's easy for some people in a group to clash with others. They can develop internal conflicts because everyone has their own ideas on what to do and how to do it.

DISC assessments review the ways in which people act in team-based and high-pressure situations. They identify the fears and concerns that employees have plus what motivates them.

More importantly, they see how well groups of people can respond to commands that are given to them. Some people, particularly Dominant ones, aren't as willing to take commands. Others are receptive and will do anything.

The DISC test will help you figure out what motivates your employees. You'll learn why they work like they do and what they want most out of the workplace.

It Meets the Needs of People

The DISC assessment does not focus on intelligence. Rather, it places an emphasis on how well people work within a group. It acknowledges that every person in the workplace is an individual with their own influences and interests.

An assessment will review group members based on the following vital points:

- How well people get along with each other;

- Whether or not co-workers are looking for some kind of power in the workplace;

- How organised those people can be;

- Whether or not they want to do things the same way all the time;

- How well people can talk with one another;

- Loyalty and what it takes to stray from it;

Everyone has their own ideas on how people will behave. The DISC test helps you see just what others can do in various situations.

A Focus On Relationships

Everyone behaves in a variety of ways. Some people argue that opposite personalities attract each other. However, this is not always the case.

The problem with many groups is that they contain people whose personalities clash with each other. Much of this is because they have various attributes that can cause their relationships with one another to weaken. This is where the DISC test can come in handy.

Unlike many other similar tests used to review personalities (Myers-Briggs, etc.), the DISC test places more of a focus on relationships. It reviews how people get along with each other, focusing on whether or not conflicts could develop. The goal is to create a sense of harmony within a larger group.

The four key behavioural types in the DISC test have their own fears and worries. These include the fear of failure, not being organised or just not having any focus. The motivating factors for why they do certain things can also be revealed. The DISC test identifies the concerns people have and finds out which ones are not compatible with one another.

Growth Must be Managed

It's easy for a business to start growing. However, it can be challenging for anyone to keep that rate of growth at a consistent level.

Part of this growth entails helping employees to advance and evolve within the workplace. The DISC assessment program will help people understand how to take care of that growth over time.

The DISC assessment helps to determine how a workforce is to evolve. Specifically, it will review individual employees based on whether or not they work better in certain situations or roles within the organisation. This in turn facilitates decisions on who should be promoted to leadership positions or at least which supporting roles people are to take.

It also helps in determining which members should be added to a group over time. Groups can evolve to include more people. This test can help review the growth rate of the group to determine if it's working well as it is or if more changes need to be made.

Reviewing Emotional Intelligence

While the DISC process is not about seeing how smart a person is, it does take a closer look at one aspect of intelligence. It looks at the emotional quotients of employees.

Emotional intelligence refers to how well a person can handle his or her thoughts. This includes a look into how well the person acts. Part of this entails whether a person understands what they are doing. This measurement reflects how well someone can answer questions.

The emotional intelligence of a person is measured through three critical concepts:

1. What someone does;

2. Why that person does it;

3. How it is done;

It delves deeper into how people behave and respond to certain situations. It especially reviews whether or not a person is aware of why they do what they do.

The DISC process goes into many critical concepts that relate to emotional intelligence:

- How aware a person is of what happens in a particular environment;

- How that person can control impulses; that is, it's about thinking before acting;

- Passion for the job;

- Empathy towards other workers;

- How well someone can build relationships;

- How far ahead a person is thinking;

By using this, it is easy to figure out the rationale that someone has. This in turn makes it easier to choose a group for that person.

This analytical test holds the key to creating the best possible team in the workplace. To start, we will talk about how the DISC process works and what it means in general.

Chapter 2 – What is DISC?

The DISC assessment process is crucial to effective business-planning. It determines what personal and emotional skills people have. These include attributes inherent within particular workplace situations.

Every individual attribute that is held by individuals in the workplace makes a difference. Some people are focused on goals. Others are focused on people. Some will be fast-paced while others are patient and willing to take their time.

The DISC test is designed to determine which characteristics these people hold. Careful reviewing of this will enable you to be more successful.

What It Means

This testing format helps by focusing on many characteristics. These attributes are essential to any worker. They determine how well someone can work and the attitudes a person holds.

The DISC term refers four main attributes that are measured within the assessment. These are attributes that will be DISCussed in further detail in the next chapter.

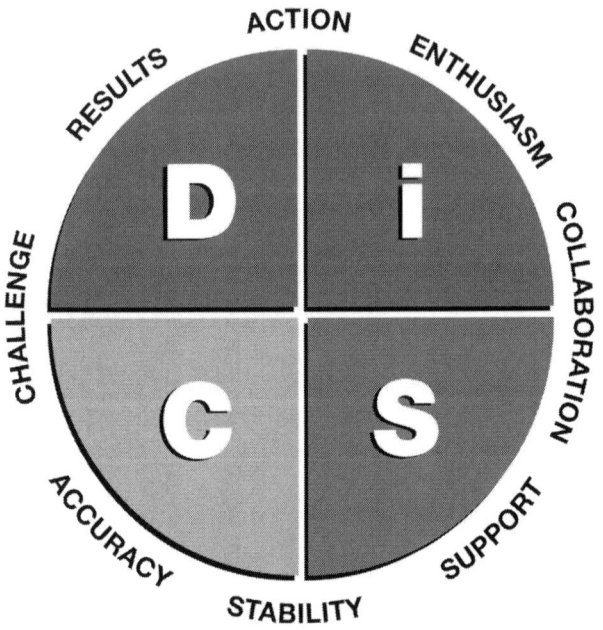

The four attributes used here are as follows:

1. **Dominant**

Direct and demanding, a dominant person focusing on doing things right and directly.

A Dominant person will do anything to have power. This person wants to be in charge and will tell people what's right and wrong as desired. Dominant people don't like to lose their powers either.

2. **Influence**

The influential person inspires people and is very persuasive and friendly.

Influential people are willing to talk with others. They want to show that they care. They especially like showing off their social skills.

3. **Steady**

Steady people are supportive and are always willing to go with the flow.

Steady people are frequently patient and aren't too concerned about being perfect. They also care about their wellbeing. In particular, they want to work in an environment where they won't be judged or pressured.

4. **Conscientious**

A conscientious person is always careful and controlled, ensuring that nothing will go wrong.

This type of person cares about the task at hand. However, that person isn't willing to hold a position of power. In fact, a Conscientious person focuses more on accuracy and precision. This includes a desire to get things right the first time even if it takes a little longer to do it.

Each of these four attributes is based on the attitudes that people have and what motivates them. People can identify with multiple attributes but in most cases only one will be dominant over the others. For instance, a person could have high steady and conscientious scores, thus being labeled as a perfectionist.

These four attributes are based on such points as:

- How much power a person feels he or she has over a situation;

- The competitive nature of that person;

- How willing they are to listen to others and go along with pre-existing plans;

- Instincts and decision-making processes;

- Ability to respond to different challenges;

- Response to change;

- Are they task-oriented or people-oriented?

- Are they patient?

- The types of schedules they have;

- The overall standards that people hold; this includes whether or not someone is willing to be imperfect;

Businesses take the DISC review process very seriously. They want employees that can handle various situations with care. The test determines what situations people can actually thrive in.

In fact, much of what goes on in this test can be attributed to two interesting measurements. These are known as drives.

The Motor Drive

The DISC model is based on two crucial drives. These are the motor and compass drives. Let's talk first about the motor drive, or the pace drive as it is sometimes called.

The motor drive refers to how well a person interacts with others. It also covers how quickly that person is willing to work.

Interactions

Interactions are crucial to the workplace. But not all people are willing to talk with others.

The **dominant and influential people are more outgoing.** They want to talk with others and share their ideas with them. They don't like to be alone; they want others around to make work varied.

Meanwhile, **the steady and conscientious people are more private.** While they often don't mind working with other like-minded people, they don't really care much about interacting with others. The lack of people in the environment also ensures that these folks are more focused on what they're doing.

Pace of Work

The pace of work relates to how quickly people work. **Dominant and influential people are a little more fast-paced.** They are active, fast and excited. They will do anything quickly and don't like to be bored.

Steady and conscientious people aren't as quick. They tend to take more time with their work. They want to focus on accuracy and care. They don't mind if they miss deadlines; they'll try and meet their deadlines but they won't always get there.

Compass Drive

The compass drive, or the priority drive, is the second drive. This places an emphasis on two different people

– those who focus on tasks and those who stick with people.

Task Focus

One half of the compass drive is the focus on getting tasks done. **Dominant and Conscientious people want to finish their tasks as well as possible.** They focus mainly on getting things done as efficiently and quickly as possible.

For the dominant side, people will command others to help them achieve tasks. Conscientious people will focus on making it perfect and accurate.

Both of them concentrate on data, logic and thinking. They don't want to be led astray from the main objectives in their work. They want to complete their jobs quickly and do it well.

People Focus

The other side of the compass drive refers to paying attention to people. These include customers, co-workers, higher-ups and so forth. **Influential and Steady people stick with a focus on others over their tasks.**

People-focused workers care more about the individuals in the process. The Influential people tend to consider emotions. They try to inspire people to get up and do things or take sides. Steady people will focus more on their own wellbeing and ensuring that they don't feel under more pressure than necessary.

How is the Screening Process Handled?

The DISC screening process is often done before a person is hired. It is also commonly used during periods of rapid growth or company restructure. Other employers will perform the test before a major project in the workplace starts up. Whatever the motivator, it is done to ensure that the right employees are in the right roles.

Specifically, the DISC test uses a series of steps to figure out if someone is suitable for a project:

1. A person will be given a questionnaire that highlights their behaviours. In most cases the questionnaire will entail statements that someone can agree with or disagree with.

2. The person will have to answer the questions based on whether they agree or disagree with the various statements listed in the test.

3. The answers can then be graded. You can do this by hand, provided that you have a full grading system available. But it's usually easier for a computer program to tally up all the totals.

4. The review will then judge a person's attributes based on the responses that were made. Each answer will influence the total score a person can get for all four attributes.

The scores are all based on how intense a person is towards a particular behaviour. That is, a person with a higher positive score will have a better total.

Tests Can be Organised Well

Try to ensure the test is treated seriously and approached in a professional manner by all. Those taking the test should not feel they are being judged on their answers and should feel able to give honest answers. Fortunately, the nature of the DISC test makes it easy to organise.

There are no limits as to how many questions can go into a DISC test. It is best to keep these questions as varied as possible. We will talk more about the questions that are often used later in this guide.

The test-takers should not feel pressured to answer questions in a certain way. There are **no right or wrong answers** in this test. Everyone who takes it should be encouraged to answer in as honest and sincere a manner as possible. There's no need to worry about people getting confused or being pushed into giving answers of a certain type.

In addition, the questions can be organised in any way you like. They can be yes or no questions, multiple-choice questions or ones that require selections being organised from most to least preferable or vice versa. The key is to have questions that are straightforward and easy to understand.

These questions will also be scored based on specific attributes. Each individual question can feature its own series of point values. You can even change the points to your liking. There are no limits to how many points you can use. Again, this is something that will be DISCussed later in this book.

Easy to Use On Anyone

One key advantage of the DISC test is that anyone can take it. You don't even have to know much about someone to gather new insights. You just have to administer the test.

The DISC test is detailed enough that it will give you information on how someone works and why that person does certain things. It focuses not only on past events but also on the present.

Also, it does not focus on job-specific skills. It focuses on attitudes and personal values. These can predict the possible skills that one might have.

In short, the DISC test isn't something that is overly technical. Anyone can take the DISC test. You could take it right now if you wanted to.

When Can it be Used?

One popular feature of the DISC test is that it is highly versatile. Naturally, it can be used in any situation where you need to learn about the underlying features and attitudes of individuals in the workplace.

However, because we want to have the best possible people in the workplace, the DISC test will help you figure out if the people you've got now are the right ones or if you need some special help.

A DISC test can be used in many situations:

When Hiring People

There are often times when a business has to hire new people. This is to not only have enough people to undertake work, but also to find people who can actually take on a specific role.

An employer can find new people who meet certain DISC characteristics at any time. The test is often used to keep the workforce varied or to at least see that the newest hires will fit in with particular routines. This can work for as many people as necessary.

But the DISC test was not only designed as a pre-employment screening test. The use of the test has evolved to where more employers are using it for screening purposes.

The DISC test could also determine which employees are no longer required in specific positions. However, it is not recommended as a means to purge employees purely because they have a specific DISC result. In fact, it could be dangerous from a legal standpoint for you to do that. Those employees can just be placed into different situations.

Remember though that while the DISC test can predict what people will do, it doesn't mean that these people will definitely act that way. Everyone is able to perform within all areas of the DISC spectrum, it just takes DISCipline and energy to drag ourselves out of our preferred behavioural style. Employees will be happier in roles that allow them to work in their natural behavioural style. It is also worth remembering that under pressure, we generally all revert to type; we use all our energy to deal with the pressure so have little left to act in a different behavioural style.

When Looking to Set Up Projects

The projects in a workplace are often varied. Some projects are designed to improve financial organisation. Others are dedicated to creating a new physical space for work or for developing a new market to sell to new clients.

The most important part of starting a project involves seeing that the people who will work on it are good enough for the job. All employees must be skilled so they can easily carry out their tasks as required. A DISC test will determine who should be assigned to a project and who should avoid it in general.

A project group could be working together for weeks, months or even years. So the need to establish a group the right way is critical or else a bunch of members that cannot interact well with each other will be stuck together for far too long, and your project will founder and staff may quit.

It's especially crucial to test potential leaders this way. It can be a useful way to find new leaders from within the organisation through this process. You could even figure out which staff members have confidence in their abilities. More importantly, you'll see who has more control over any situation or circumstance.

When Getting Promotions Ready

Only the best employees can get promotions. The best and most prominent positions will go to those who have proven themselves to be proficient in their jobs.

It can take years of experience and hard work to get a promotion. Still, there are times when one person will be a more appropriate candidate for promotion than others. That is, even a person who is less experienced can qualify for a promotion over someone who has more knowledge. This is not out of personal preference; it is out of understanding the attributes someone has.

A person with the right attributes should have excellent people-skills and a good record of project completion.

That person will be more appropriate for promotion. Of course, the reasons an employer has for offering promotion will vary; the DISC test simply makes it easier for that employer to make decisions on who will work most easily in each type of leadership role.

Learning About Yourself

If you are planning on testing others, it seems only fair that you take the test yourself. It not only gives you an understanding for what it is like to face the testing process, but provides invaluable insights about your own working style and how best to communicate with the other work styles in your team.

You'll learn about how you respond to conflicts and how you're motivated. You will especially see what causes stress in your life and why it's a problem. This all goes towards problem solving; it reviews how well people respond to different problems.

You will even see who you would work with the best. This refers to how well you interact with others and why some people are easier to be around.

Of course, you should only complete a DISC test that you haven't seen yet. You can't just take your own test – you already know how the scoring works. That could influence your answers and give you a false result.

Enhancing Customer Support

Businesses often use the DISC assessment as a means of figuring out who's best at getting in touch with customers. The customer is the lifeblood of any business. A business with employees that don't know how to interact appropriately with customers will certainly fail. Customers want to do business with those who understand their needs and aren't stubborn, uninterested or pushy in their approach.

More importantly, a business needs employees who can persuade customers and make them feel at home. The DISC test demonstrates those who are best suited to directly working with customers.

Training Purposes

Training can make a difference in the workplace. It helps employees understand what needs to be done and gives them the tools to do it.

The DISC assessment helps businesses understand what tendencies certain workers have. This in turn allows the business to adjust its training programs based on what skills staff members need.

In turn this will create a more efficient workforce. The training process must be utilised carefully and with the needs of the employees in mind.

Effectively Manage and Implement Change

There's always a necessity to figure out how well a business adapts to change. Changes can relate to new ownership or leadership, new markets, a new location or brand new duties and resources. However not everyone copes well with change. Some take longer to embrace it.

The DISC test will determine who is more receptive to change. This will include those who aren't going to handle changes well.

Who Uses This?

The DISC assessment is used in a variety of places. It is valuable in large organisations. It's to find potential employees and determine who should be promoted or placed into certain teams.

It's also used by non-profit groups. It determines who is best at organising events and keeping projects on track.

Even hospitals, churches, mental health facilities and schools will use the DISC assessment on some people. It helps to understand the behaviours people have and how their behaviour can influence physical or mental decisions. This in turn allows for an understanding of what someone is comfortable doing and why that is.

Differences Between DISC and Myers-Briggs

The Myers-Briggs test is often compared with the DISC test. This test is also an assessment of people. It reviews attitudes and behaviours just like the DISC test.

Still, the DISC test is different from the Myers-Briggs test. Here are a few of the key reasons why.

How People Do Things

The Myers-Briggs test reviews how people think about the world. It's about how people see things and observe them.

The DISC test focuses instead on how people do things. It is about the behaviours people use when doing them. It is not just about the thought process. It's about what it is that makes such thoughts happen.

How People Adapt

The DISC and Myers-Briggs tests both take a look at how people act. However, the Myers-Briggs test focuses on how people act based on what they do in familiar places, for example at home or in familiar settings.

The DISC test moves well beyond the ways how people act at home. It also looks into how people behave in situations that they are not familiar with. That is, it entails how people adapt to change and new events.

Variety of Questions

The Myers-Briggs test has only one particular type of question. This is the yes-no question. It forces people into an extremely limited series of possible answers.

The DISC test can potentially utilise this option. However, it will use a greater variety of questions, particularly ones that entail rankings. You will learn more about the variety of questions in the DISC test later in this guide.

Scoring Compares You to Others

The scoring used in the DISC process is also treated differently. The scoring is based heavily on a person's behavioural style. It is generated based on the scores one attains over a few questions.

Let's say that you took the test yourself. You'd learn more about yourself right away. However, this test will let you do more than just that.

In addition to learning your skills, the test will compare your results with the scores of other people. That is, it concentrates on the averages that people are expected to obtain within the test. This is based on all the different characteristics that are to be measured. This is not like the setting the Myers-Briggs test uses. That test tends to work with only a limited point total.

The standards used are based on the different segments that people can be placed in. These segments are divided based on the number of points given to each category. Some segments have higher point totals than others. Either way, the scores that you get will influence your ranking and make you look like a more favourable person for many positions.

A Greater Variance

There's a much greater variance that can come about within the DISC test. The DISC test will allow you to ask as many questions as you want. You will have full control over how the test is organised and the form the questions take. It's generally best to be as varied and thorough as possible if you want to get the best out of the test.

The DISC test will ensure it checks every aspect of a person's character. This is not limited to a few concepts. It goes through a person's entire behavioural system.

A Non-Judgmental Exercise

The most important benefit of the DISC test is that it doesn't criticise anyone who takes it. The DISC test focuses less on how much someone knows and more on what someone thinks. It pays attention to the emotional and personal side of one's life, not on value judgements.

The DISC test concentrates on understanding what makes people tick. It's about influences and what makes a person act in a certain way.

Granted, you could adjust the DISC test to create questions that might reflect your particular workplace. However, these should be questions that focus less on abilities and more on one's beliefs or values.

Overall, the DISC test will give you the answers you need about anyone in the workplace. But what is it about the four key attributes that make them so critical? Let's take a look in the next chapter.

DOMINANT

Priorities: getting immediate results, taking action, challenging self and others

Motivated by: power and authority, competition, winning, success

Fears: loss of control, being taken advantage of, vulnerability

You will notice: self confidence, directness, forcefulness, risk taking

Limitations: lack of concern for others, impatience, insensitivity

INFLUENCE

Priorities: expressing enthusiasm, taking action, encouraging collaboration

Motivated by: social recognition, group activities, good relationships

Fears: social rejection, disapproval, loss of influence, being ignored

You will notice: charm, enthusiasm sociability, optimism, talkativeness

Limitations: impulsiveness, disorganisation, lack of follow through

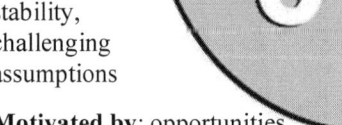

Priorities: accuracy, maintaining stability, challenging assumptions

Motivated by: opportunities to use expertise or gain knowledge, attention to quality

Fears: criticism, being wrong

You will notice: precision, analysis, scepticism, reserve, quiet

Limitations: overly critical, tendency to overanalyse, isolates

CONCIENTIOUSNESS

Priorities: giving support, maintain stability, collaboration

Motivated by: stable environments, appreciation, cooperation, opportunities to help

Fears: loss of stability, change, loss of harmony, offending others

You will notice: patience, team player, calm approach, humility

Limitations: overly accommodating, indecisiveness

STEADY

Chapter 3 – A Deeper Look at the Four Key Points

You've always wanted to know the inner workings of your employees – but did you know they could all be summarised by four simple words?

Dominance, influence, steady and conscientious – they may sound deceptively simple but they can mean everything to your business. They each come with their own special set of mental constants.

The DISC process is devoted to using these four critical points to determine how well a person can respond to certain events and activities. It ensures that all employees are analysed clearly and properly.

Most importantly, this helps you to figure out who's the most suitable for individual positions. It takes a look at who's responsible, who's willing to stick around in the background and who's more emotional. Some are focused on details and others just want to keep their routines as consistent as possible.

Let's take a closer look at all of these points. As you will see, these people have their own traits and influences. They also have their own drawbacks but you can still get in touch with someone and be on that person's level.

Dominance

The first aspect of the DISC assessment entails the dominance that some people have. A dominant person is one that **is more interested in leading people in different tasks.** That person wants to have as much power as possible and is not keen on following the commands of others.

Dominance entails having control; a dominant person will wrestle as much control in a situation as possible.

Dominant people are true leaders. They want as much control of their situations as possible. They're willing to go the extra mile for it and want to get straight to the point. They don't like those who delay or dally.

Always full of energy, a dominant person is more concerned about getting things done than anything else. This person is decisive and persistent.

A dominant person will want to take a full grip of any given situation. A person who is not in control will be far from dominant.

Dominant people care about being high-up and in a strong position. Dominant people want to move forward.

A Focus on Results

Dominant people like to be in power but one critical concept that a dominant person holds is the desire to get the best possible result. A dominant person will work as hard as possible to achieve their objectives and will do what it takes to get there:

- A dominant person will think about the bottom line above all else. While some smaller tasks can be important, it is the big picture that the dominant person will consider.

- Time frames are also reviewed by a dominant figure. This includes a look at how easily a project can be completed within a certain period of time. Schedules for completing tasks are often drafted by dominant people to try and keep everyone on track.

- Dominant people are also highly direct and don't like to delay things or beat about the bush.

- An aggressive nature will also be exhibited. That is, the dominant person will be adamant on ensuring that certain results are achieved regardless of the way they are done.

Dominant people care about results because they want to show the world that they know what they are capable of. They want to be taken seriously.

Highly Confident

Dominant people are especially **confident about who they are.** They want to confirm their confidence by working as hard as possible to find solutions to practically any problem that will show up.

Confident people like these will do what they can to succeed:

- They will take a look at the problems that occur and work as hard as possible to find solutions to them.

- Any task will be prepared based more on what can happen and the benefits that will come about above all else. The negatives are not going to be focused upon as they would be too limiting. Negative people will also shut down lines of thought from others.

- They will also check on every individual avenue that can be used to solve problems, sometimes going as far as to take extraordinary risks just to reach certain goals.

- There's also a tendency among dominant people to avoid thinking about the bad things that can come about in a project.

Concerns for Such People

While a dominant person should be someone who has control over what is done, there can still be some common problems in people who are dominant:

- Dominant people are afraid to lose power. They don't want to be undermined by others.

- Dominant people are often not all that concerned about others. They aren't aware of the needs of others and will become impatient if things don't go according to plan.

- Dominant people don't want to think about negative things or even the problems that can come about if certain things are done. This can lead to ignoring vital possibilities that should be taken into account; a dominant person only tends to focus on the good things that can happen and may not take a wholly realistic view.

- People who delay things, those are uncertain about themselves and people who have no idea what to do in a situation are frustrating to dominant workers. Dominant people don't like to bear with those make a task harder and more complicated than they believe necessary.

How to Interact with a Dominant Person

People in the workplace can easily support a dominant person by using a few sensible ideas:

- People need to respect those who are dominant. This is to keep conflicts from developing.

- People should also have evidence to support any arguments or points they want to make with dominant people.

- Brevity is crucial; DISCussions with dominant people must be to the point.

- A strong focus is also required. Dominant people do not like it when people wander away from the main topic. They demand concentration in everything that they do.

Dominant people are always looking to find ways to be in charge. They will always **go after the bottom line.**

Influence

Have you ever seen stories about people who inspire others? Perhaps you have seen stories about a child being a major influence the life of a professional athlete or politician. People who don't have lots of power can still be influential. They can get people to understand what they want to do. They can inspire others to carry out enormous undertakings on their behalf.

Influence can mean a lot to most of us. In fact, that's what the second attribute is about. It's about knowing how to get people to learn more and to side with one viewpoint over another

The I in the DISC test refers to the influence that someone can hold. An influential person is **more interested in getting people to feel better about the situations they are in.** This type of person will concentrate especially on trying to create **a sense of unity** in whatever is going on.

Influential people like to interact with others. They always place greater consideration of the people they work with than the tasks they are to complete.

An influential person can also work hard to persuade people. They will do anything to get people to agree upon something.

This is all done with a strong sense of optimism. The problems in the workplace aren't obstacles to the influential employee – they are opportunities just waiting to be DISCovered.

The Centre of Attention

One significant part of an influential person comes from one's desire to be the centre of attention. That is, a person will do whatever it takes to be the focal point within a team. In addition, the influential person will commonly:

- Do anything to improve the sense of optimism within the workplace. This includes establishing a sense of enthusiasm among team members.

- Be persuasive. Persuasion is a critical part of using influence; it entails getting people to side with a particular viewpoint above all else.

- Emphasise the emotional aspect of a job.

- Willing to engage in DISCussion. They will always talk it out with others. This can entail both working to resolve issues and attempting to persuade people into seeing that certain concepts can end up being brighter and more advantageous than others.

- Be more concerned about popularity than others.

These attributes are used by an influential person to find ways to get people to pay attention and do things in a particular manner. The control held by an influential person could make a major impact on anyone's behaviour.

Get People to Work Together

Togetherness is a critical part of any project in the workplace. An influential person will do everything to try and get people to work together without any debates or arguments.

The influential figure in the workplace will especially concentrate on being sociable and talkative. This includes a desire to get everyone in the workplace to really be happy with whatever is happening here.

Part of this can even include a sense of spontaneity. This entails getting people to think about what they can do at any time while being ready to change things around on a whim if desired. It's about not only completing tasks but also ensuring that people are on the same page and willing to work together in any situation.

Concerns About the Influential Worker

While the influential worker will do what he or she can to make people feel great about a situation and to work together, there are some problems that will be prevalent in such a worker as this:

- An influential worker will not be likely to stay as organised as others in the workplace.

- It's often tough for some influential workers to speak directly to others. They often try to avoid confrontation, plain-speaking and will sugarcoat the truth; they are often reluctant to say anything critical or negative.

- Sometimes a person like this isn't totally skilled in some necessary field. That person can struggle to learn new tasks or even avoid some of the more technical aspects of whatever has to be done at a given time.

- Influential workers don't like it when they don't get much of a say over what to do.

- A lack of spontaneity can especially make such a worker feel unwelcome.

- Some influential workers are not comfortable with negative ideas. They will try and sidestep them where possible, ignoring serious threats that could make a situation worse if not confronted head-on.

Interacting with an Influential Person

Those who want to interact with an influential person can do the following:

- It's important to be sociable with an influential person. This is necessary to build a good relationship.

- Not much time should be spent on the details during a conversation.

- Anything that is DISCussed has to be translated into actions that are easy to follow.

- Accomplishments should also be recognised.

Influential people want attention but in a good way. They want to **create a positive and comfortable environment for all.**

Steady

Not all workers willingly seek to be the centre of attention. Some people are more willing to submit to ideas than others. These are people known as steady employees.

We've all heard that story about 'slow and steady' winning the race. Well, some people prefer to stick with this adage and live by it. This is where steady people, or at least those who score steady on the DISC test, come into play.

They are people who want to keep themselves under control. They will always make an effort to see that nothing will go wrong in the workplace. In particular, steadiness is a part of the DISC review that entails one's willingness to **accommodate the needs of**

others without complaint. That is, the steady person is not going to try and work too hard to change things.

A steady employee is one who listens to people and is loyal to whomever is leading a project. Think of a steady person as the polar opposite of a dominant one. The steady person is not only fine with commands being given but is also willing to stick with those commands through thick and thin.

In fact, it is often hard for steady people to find friends. They tend to keep their relationships as close as possible when they do find those friends.

Patience and Control

Heading back to the tortoise and hare story, the tortoise was patient and controlled. He won the race because he was careful. Steady people believe that this can be carried over into the real world. That is, anyone can win by being patient. Rushing the project is not going to do anyone any good.

Patience and control are often tough for some people to live with but they are virtues that must be followed in the workplace regardless of that. A steady employee is one that will not fear the passage of time; rather, that person will be focused on being controlled and willing to go along with everything someone else has planned.

In particular, the steady person is willing to accept others. That person is not going to be judgmental. The person will not even want to know why someone acts in any particular way.

The most important point about patience is calmness. The steady person is always calm and doesn't easily become stressed by events. In fact, this lack of stress helps the person to remain at ease.

Trustworthiness Is Crucial

A steady employee will prefer many things in the work environment. Much of this entails the desire to create a strong and powerful sense of trust in the workplace. Trustworthiness is a common and valuable trait in the steady employee:

- A steady employee prefers it when the work environment is stable and predictable.

- Steady employees also like it when the leadership status quo is the same or at least does not change too much or too often.

- Repetition is a good thing in the eyes of steady employees. They are okay with doing the same things all the time. They are great for repetitive and continuing tasks.

- This kind of employee will not be confrontational or argumentative.

- Loyalty and trustworthiness are the most important things that these people both offer and value in others. This includes a desire to understand what goes on in a variety of situations.

- Steady employees will always listen to other people. They will want to know more about what they can do, how to do it and why it is so important.

Concerns Over Steady Employees

The problems that often occur with the steady employee are important ones that have to be considered with care:

- Such employees are not comfortable with sudden change.

- It may take them a while to get used to new members of staff, particularly in positions of authority.

- It can be easy for an employee like this to lose track of things if any major changes develop quickly.

- Some people could also work a little slower than others. They generally work with highly systematic processes to resolve certain situations.

- They need more time to prepare for change and take longer to adjust themselves after changes take place. This will often slow down some processes or delay work.

- Steady employees will often struggle to confront other people. It is a challenge to try and get people to change their minds or to even adjust whatever is going on in the workplace. Sometimes they will put up with uncomfortable situations for a long period of time.

- The process of adapting to new things is often a struggle for steady people.

- Some people trust too much. They blindly follow anything someone says regardless of whether it's a sensible or illogical idea. They are apt to agree with everything they are asked to do, and can become overwhelmed.

Connecting with Steady People

Steady people are easy to get along with provided you know what to do. There are many things that you can do to keep a connection with a steady person strong:

- Be interested in them and friendly.

- Give a steady person extra time to adjust to any changes that come about.

- Don't pressure or hurry a steady person too much. That would only cause the person to go too fast and make mistakes.

- Any new ideas must be introduced carefully, slowly and in an easy-to-understand way.

Steady people aren't going to be rushed into anything. They are **sincere, comfortable and dependable.**

Conscientious

The fourth and final characteristic of many people entails the art of being conscientious. A conscientious employee is one that is **detailed, orderly and willing to focus on the task at hand.**

The conscientious person will be cautious. The like to do things to a system and always in order. The like full and detailed instructions so they have a full understanding of how something is to be done.

In addition, they will make every effort to **do things right and in a thorough and careful manner.** They will figure out what can be done to make things right the first time around. This person is logical and fact-based while being a stickler for following the rules.

Such a person can be seen as the polar opposite of the influential person. Whereas the influential person will focus more on getting people to feel motivated and ready, the conscientious person will instead concentrate on finding ways to keep the situation under control while paying more attention to the task that must be completed rather than the employees who will handle it.

Also, such people will work hard to **get all people in a group to be on the same page.** That is, they want everyone to be fully aware of how certain tasks are to be run, thus potentially getting everyone to be more efficient and productive.

Care and Caution

A conscientious person has in any situation an overriding desire to accomplish their tasks in a careful manner. In particular, a conscientious person will be concerned with **independence and control.** This means that by working on a project with few outside factors getting in the way, it is be easier to take ownership of a task and ensure control of it, thereby accomplishing completion of that task in the manner they deem best.

Commonplace Concerns

The concerns that can show in a person who focuses on being conscientious are noteworthy issues that can prevent them from working well with others:

- Some conscientious people are withdrawn and distant. They don't want to share their feelings with others.

- The schedules that conscientious people hold are rigid. That is, they aren't willing to adjust things too often. Anything new that comes about will upset their schedule and overall plans.

- Some conscientious people will be overly critical of others. This is especially the case with people who think a little too far outside the box.

- Conscientious people will also be less likely to trust others in the workplace. They have difficulty trusting the routines of others and may consider the procedures others choose are totally wrong and inaccurate. This does not mean that a conscientious person cannot have friends; such a person will often have a few very close friends.

- Conscientious people hate being wrong. They will do anything to prove that they're right. They can find themselves backed into a corner if they too rigidly refuse to accept their mistakes.

- While these people are always willing to stick with certain tasks for as long as required, they will also find it difficult to switch to other tasks as priorities change. They may have a tendency to micro-manage.

- Anything that is too vague or non-specific will not be welcomed by the conscientious person who prefers detailed requests and measurable results.

Communicating with a Conscientious Person

While it's true that a conscientious person is private and excessively logical, there are ways to make working with them a little easier for everyone. Several things can be done when talking to such a person:

- Be as logical and clear as possible. Conscientious people often ask why more than others.

- Be patient and prepared; try not to improvise or make impulsive decisions.

- Explain things in a logical manner and link them to the bigger picture.

- Try to let a conscientious person know about changes or other new ideas ahead of time. Don't upset them with sudden changes or last-minute requests.

Like a dominant person, a conscientious person will want to do things well. However, the conscientious will go one step further. That person will **focus on accuracy and knowledge with a fear of failure.**

All four parties are unique in their own ways. They must all be reviewed carefully as they are gifted in different tasks and routines. It is essential to try to accommodate everyone to create consistency and control.

Chapter 4 – Patterns to Find

A DISC test will generally find out just which of these four attributes fully describes an individual. Most people will score well on two different attributes, although one is usually higher. These are the Primary and Secondary attributes that go to making up a persons individual style. The two different attributes might even appear to be polar opposites; one attribute could score very high and the other could be just about nonexistent.

Have you ever read that *Divergent* book series? The series said that everyone in its universe had to meet a certain characteristic. However, some people would meet many characteristics in a number of attributes.

The real world is different from the one Veronica Roth created. In the *Divergent* world, you could be in trouble for not exclusively fitting into one group. In our world, you could be an asset if you score well on more than just one attribute in the DISC test.

You need to measure the results in your DISC tests as carefully as possible. The answers that people give will influence their scores by adding or subtracting points within certain attributes.

This is normally done by hand, which can be tedious. Fortunately, a computer program can help you out by taking care of those calculations for you.

From this, you will get a clear display of the results. The results of a DISC assessment will be laid out in a simple chart design. This features reviews of each individual attribute. That is, there are four dots on the chart and the lines will go up and down depending on what the results of the test were.

The results are organised based on certain point totals that will vary from one test to another. Your results will also be organised within sections.

This gives you a full overview of anyone's skills and attributes. You might be surprised at what some people answer within this test and how their results turn out.

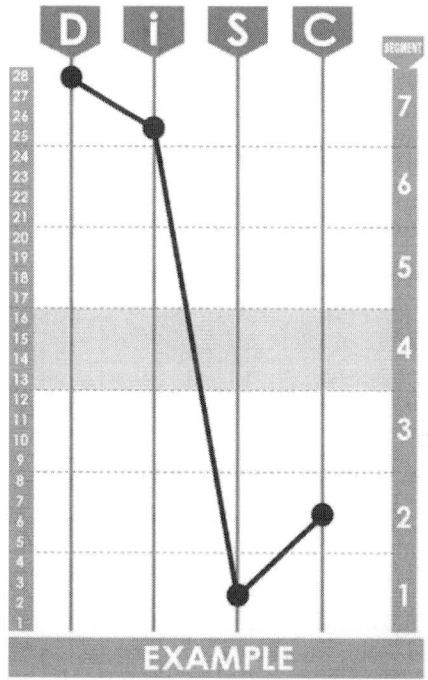

This is an example of how the DISC test readout works. It features each individual attribute; the ones that are higher up are reflective of the attitudes that someone holds.

The seven segments are arranged based on the intensity of an attribute. A person who scores in the sixth or seventh segment in an attribute will have a very high total.

The fourth segment is highlighted; this is because it's the middle point. This is the dividing line between whether a person has an attribute or not.

You will find one of fifteen different patterns in your DISC results. These patterns are organised based on the particular attribute that a person favours and how that person scores on the other three.

The point of this chapter is simple – there's always a need for an entrepreneur to organise a team based on the behavioural patterns that everyone exhibits. People will behave in their own unique ways. It is vital to figure out who works best at what task and who is more compatible with others in any situation.

These fifteen patterns are divided up between each of the four key attributes. That is, there is one attribute that is more prevalent among others with the other three showing radically different results – or even similar results in some cases.

The Importance of Patterns

The patterns that you'll find are essential with regards to reviewing your employees. Patterns are designed to help you see what attitudes people hold.

In particular, patterns go deep into reviewing what opinions people hold and specifically how they will behave. While some leaders are adamant about doing what they want, they may be willing to allow for some creativity or aren't afraid to delegate things to others, for instance.

Patterns go well beyond the four key attributes in the DISC test. This looks into how a person might behave and whether or not there's more than one attribute that is their strength. This is a fascinating part of the DISC test that deserves to be explored further.

With that in mind, let's look at the many patterns that are commonly seen. These patterns are divided up based on which characteristic is the most prevalent one a test-taker holds.

Dominant Patterns

The following patterns are designed to show who hold dominant behaviours. These are people who have more control over what they want and are willing to lead.

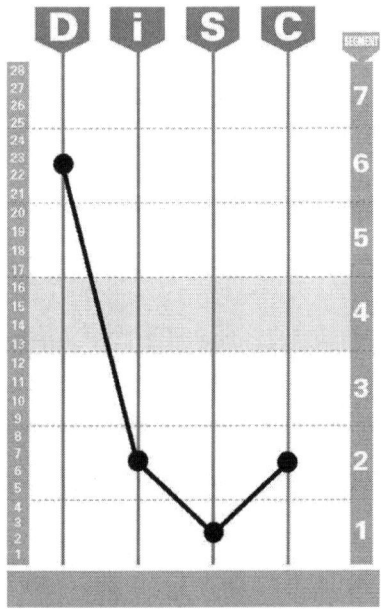

Developer

A developer will focus more on being dominant and will have a very low steadiness score.

This person is generally focused on working hard while being persistent. A developer will do anything to try and advance a cause or prove an idea.

The characteristics of a developer are as follows:

- A developer is more interested in finding solutions on their own. Such a person is willing to create new ideas.

- The developer is also direct and will keep on trying to succeed no matter how many times they fail.

- Developers tend to have high expectations.

- A developer will not be happy with those who cannot complete their objectives.

The developer will do what they can to succeed and won't be happy with failure.

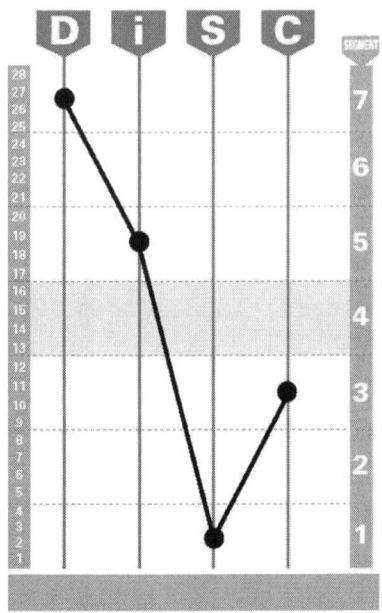

Result-Oriented

A result-oriented worker is a dominant figure who holds a high influence score but is well below average on the other two categories, particularly steadiness.

As the name suggests, a result-oriented worker will be more interested in getting the most out of a project. That person wants nothing but the best results.

A result-oriented person will exhibit these behaviours:

- They will be confident in their own abilities.

- They will also enjoy feeling independent.

- The biggest motivation of a result-oriented person is a desire to maintain control of the situation. This includes taking the lead with no one getting in the way.

- Result-oriented people can be forceful.

- This person doesn't like routines either. There's a desire to mix things up on occasion.

Anyone who is result-oriented focuses on one thing – ensuring that a project is run right and has the right outcome. Anything that doesn't work well is a problem.

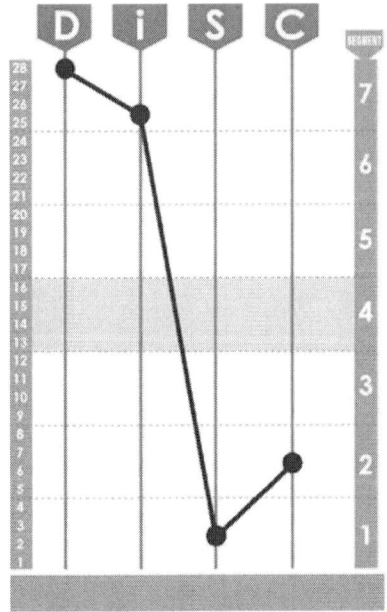

Inspirational

An inspirational person has very high dominant and influential characteristics. The other two will score very low.

An inspirational person is someone who will influence the actions that other people engage in. Inspirational people aren't willing to dominate people so much as they are willing to cooperate with them.

The points that come with an inspirational person include the following:

- They have charm and charisma.

- Inspirational people don't want to look or appear weak.

- Rewards and intimidation are often used by inspirational people.

- The biggest motivation to inspirational people is the desire to control their environment.

The most important goal of an inspirational person is to get others to feel happy. They want to be positive while making others comfortable.

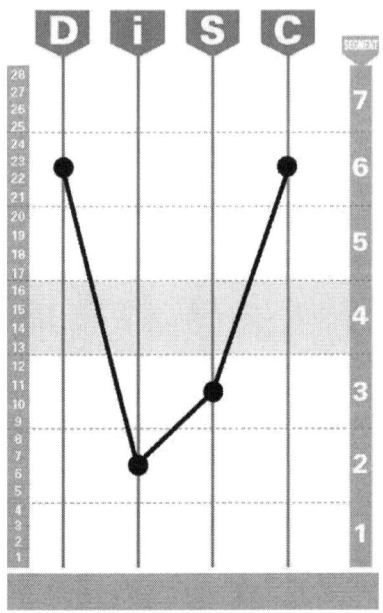

Creative

A creative person has strong dominant and conscientious scores. The influence score is very low.

Creative people are ones that want to succeed and be perfect but want to do this as soon as possible. They tend to plan things well and want to explore different ideas.

There are many great points seen in creative people:

- Creative people are often restrained from others. They are willing to go along with aggressive people.

- Creative people like to encourage positive forms of change.

- They will judge others by the way they behave or how they compete with one another.

- Routine work is boring to these people; they want to create new things and experiment.

More importantly, a creative person will see no boundaries. That person will do anything they want without thinking about what can or cannot be done. If something doesn't look like it can actually be done, the creative person will just figure out a new way.

Influential Patterns

Influential attitudes can lead to some impressive behaviours. This includes trying to get people on the same page.

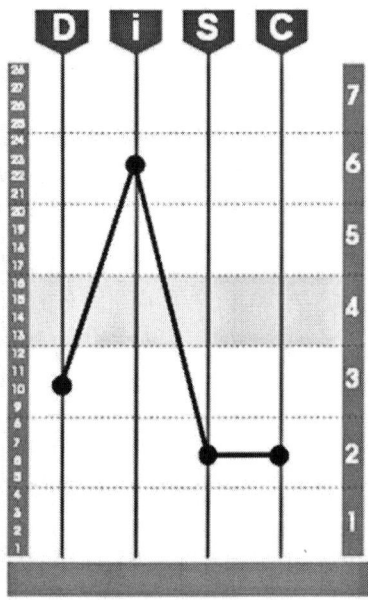

Promoter

A promoter has a high influence score and a mid-range dominant score. The other two attributes score very low.

The promoter will support others and will establish as big a market as possible. This person wants to inspire others in the group.

The following concepts will be used by a promoter:

- Promoters will do what they can to control their emotions.

- They are interested in what other people have to say.

- They also try to keep tensions under control. These include tensions from themselves and others in the group.

- Promoters are motivated by the idea of being accepted.

- Promoters are particularly good at accepting others; they are not judgmental.

Promoters like to highlight things and aren't afraid to talk with others about the many amazing positives out there. More importantly, they will sell ideas; they will let everyone know that there's no reason to be afraid of new ideas or concepts.

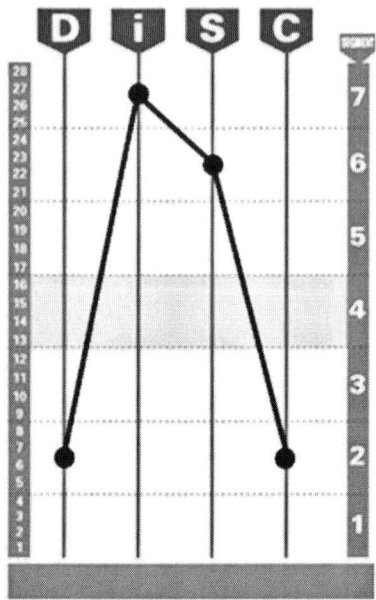

Persuader

The persuader also has a strong influence score and a mid-range dominant score. The conscientious score is low but it is slightly higher than the steady score.

A persuader will sell ideas to others. This person has ideas and wants to get people to agree upon them. Persuaders are optimistic and do their best to look great.

The points that persuaders have include the following:

- They express themselves well.

- They are easily led into bad ideas especially if stressed.

- They can organise their lives to look their best.

- Persuaders are afraid of rejection.

- Persuaders don't like routine activities.

A good example of a persuader is someone who tries to sell good and products on television. An infomercial host will do what they can to sell a concept to someone while focusing on the positive aspects of that item.

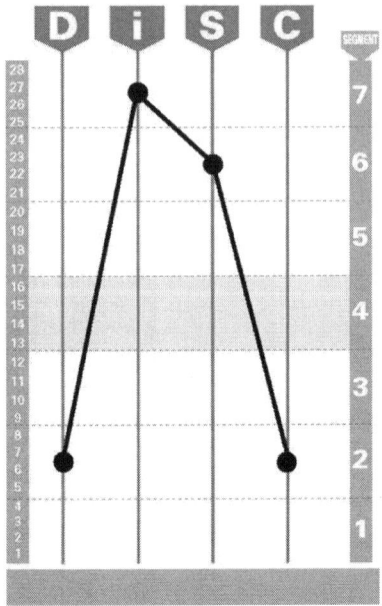

Counsellor

A Counsellor has high influence and steady scores. While the dominant and conscientious scores are very low.

Counsellors are great problems solvers. The relate to other people very well and will find people drawn to them through their compassion, understanding and sincerity. The find the good in others and are natural optimists.

You will see these traits in a cousnellor:

- Build long lasting relationships

- Good listener, willing to hear others problems without imposing their ideas

- Approachable, showing kindness and empathy to all

- Counsellors fear putting other people under pressure and tend to be overly flexible and tolerant, even when a firm hand is called for

- Respond well to compliments and recognition but will take criticism to heart

As we can assume from the name, these people make excellent counsellors. You may find this person in a professional counselling role. You will also find them in all areas of society and most workplaces, this is the person people go to when then need a shoulder to cry on or just a sympathetic ear.

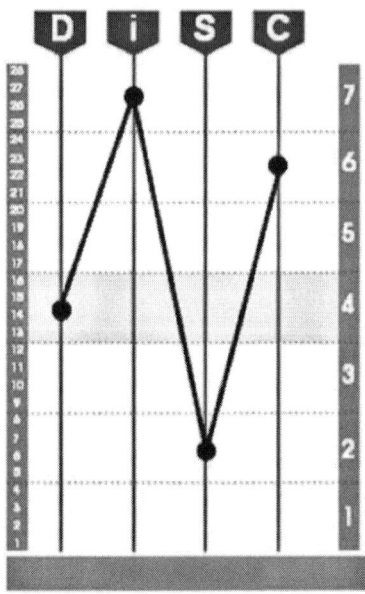

Appraiser

An appraiser has high influence and conscientious scores. The dominant score is near the middle while the steady score is very low.

Appraisers communicate quite well with people and do their best to influence others. But they retain a sense of realism.

These characteristics are common among appraisers:

- Appraisers will try to succeed every time and aren't afraid to sacrifice things to get their way.

- Appraisers don't like people who aren't going to take control or agree with them.

- Appraisers can be critical of others. They especially hate those who hold things up.

- The biggest fear of an appraiser is the risk of failure and loss.

For example we see this type of person in antique shops placing values on certain items. They are often willing to place prices on items as they see fit and don't like to delay when getting their values set up. This type of person is an appraiser and is someone who works hard to show people just why something is worth what it is.

Steady Personalities

Persistence can be important to steady personalities.
These particular results are signs of how people can do
this.

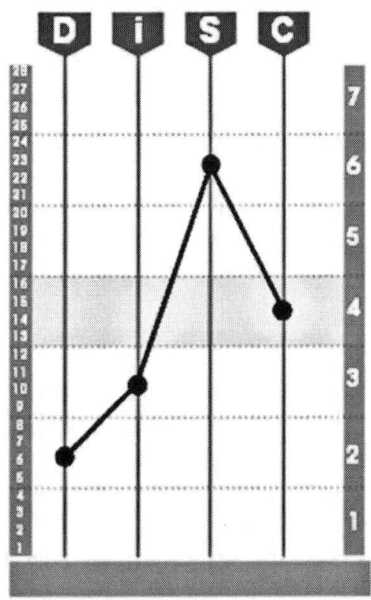

Specialist

A specialist will hold a high steady score while the
conscientious score is near the middle. The dominance
score will be very low.

A specialist is a realistic and confident person who will help others no matter what the outcome. They will do anything to establish peace and calm.

Some of the attributes of the specialist are:

- They are willing to go along with whatever others want to do. They can accommodate their schedules and resources to them.

- They prefer stable environments that are well-controlled.

- Specialists do not like change.

- Relationships are easy for specialists to develop. These are often of a lasting nature.

Of course, as the name suggests, this is a person who focuses on one main skill or activity. The truth is that a specialist does not have to just stick with one task or routine in the workplace. That person will have full control over their activities and won't be afraid to adapt to change.

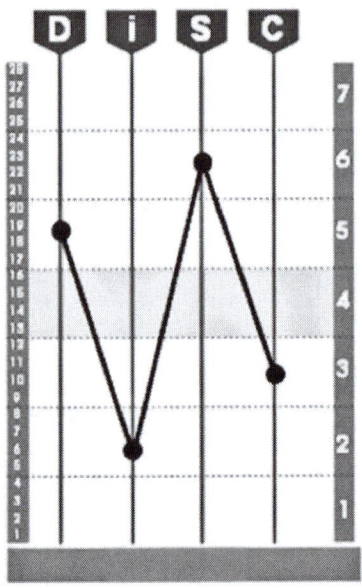

Achiever

An achiever has high steady and dominance scores. The influence score will be low.

An achiever feels highly accountable for everything they do. They feel a need to keep moving forward and to reach certain goals through persistence and effort.

Achievers can be identified by these points:

- Achievers are motivated by what they have done in the past.

- Achievers don't do anything harmful to others. However they only focus on what they think is beneficial to them.

- Achievers are deliberate and independent from others.

- They prefer to be independent; they are not willing to share their tasks and duties to others.

- They can become stressed and nervous if others around them aren't pulling their weight.

Achievers will not always succeed. However, they will do everything possible to succeed and win. They can even use the failures they had in the past to inspire themselves to do better next time. They are not going to be happy about failing but they will use them as constructive building blocks towards the future.

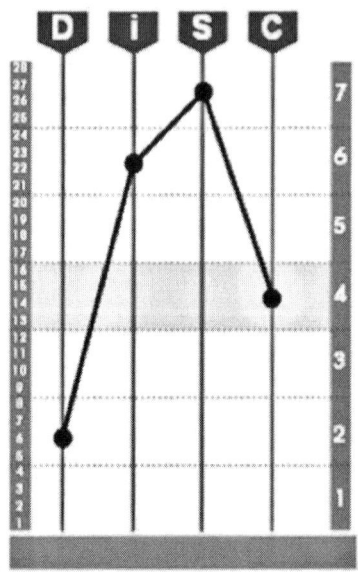

Agent

An agent will have very high steady and influence scores. Meanwhile, the dominant score is very low.

An agent will have an attitude suggesting empathy and desiring nature. They will stay with the status quo but will certainly help others to stay comfortable and to stick with the process.

Agents are identified by these features:

- Agents are quiet and non-threatening.

- Agents will accept people in their group.

- Agents will include others in their tasks.

- The agent seeks to bring harmony to any project. This includes empathising with others.

- The friendships that an agent has will directly influence decisions.

A sports agent is a good example of who fits this class – which is probably obvious as the word agent is part of their job title. A sports agent always supports their athletes and creates good relationships with them. This can even reach a point where the athlete is more trusting of their agent than the teams they are signed with.

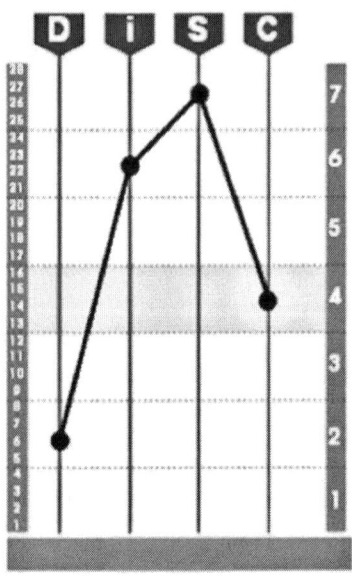

Investigator

An investigator has a high steady score and a very low influential score. The conscientious and dominance scores are in the middle.

An investigator knows what their goals are and will persist in achieving that goal. Logic and fact are in greater use than emotions.

There are many great points in investigators:

- Investigators are determined and follow through on their plans.

- Investigators are comfortable with responsibility. They are not afraid to let things work their way.

- Investigators can sometimes be unwilling to trust others. They focus too much on the head instead of the heart.

- They can hold grudges. This is especially true in times of stress.

- They don't like being criticised by others. They don't like to be involved with other people too much.

Investigators are often loners; they are often alone in what they believe. This is in spite of their willingness to succeed and win.

Conscientious Personalities

Finally, we can look at the conscientious people. These are people who focus on thoughts above all else.

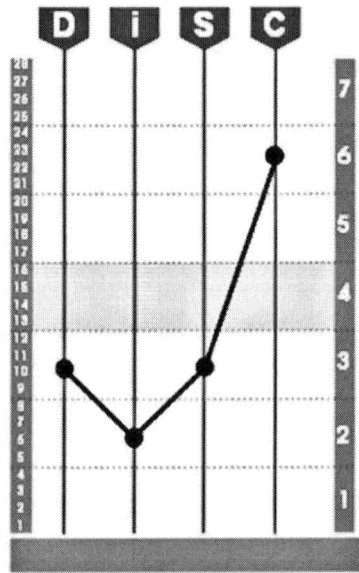

Objective Thinker

Objective Thinker personalities hold a high conscientious score, the other three attributes, especially the influence score, will be very low.

Objective thinkers concentrate on total accuracy and success. They want to be perfect and won't dwell too much on the past.

More importantly, an objective thinker is in charge of their emotions. A thinker knows what they want. In addition:

- Objective thinkers make their decisions based on logic.

- They prefer to be independent. However they are happy to work with others when the occasion demands it.

- They often analyse things a little too much.

- Their ability to gather facts and organise them is a big asset to the team.

- Objective thinkers take time to review and test every bit of evidence they can find.

Facts are more important to objective thinkers. Opinions never make much of an impression on the objective thinker, who bases their actions on evidence and logic. Opinions just make them feel misled.

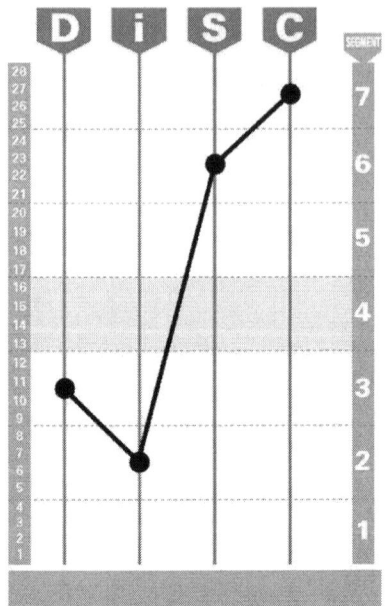

Perfectionist

Perfectionists have high conscientious and steady scores and are very low on the other two points.

Perfectionists, as the name suggests, want things to be as perfect as possible. There's no reason for doing something if it can't be done perfectly the first time around.

They prefer to keep things as consistent as possible. They are not comfortable with the unexpected or with colleagues who don't pull their weight.

Perfectionists also feature these critical aspects to their characters:

- They are reserved and careful. They don't want to rush things.

- Their standards are extremely high. Sometimes too high.

- They prefer it when they're in stable situations. They want things to stay controlled and predictable.

- Some tend to stick with things they did in the past for far too long. These include failed procedures and ideas.

- They only resort to getting help from others when all other options fail.

- They don't like hostile work environments.

The biggest problem that a perfectionist has is their fear of failure. Anything bad that happens will be a huge blow to the perfectionist's ego.

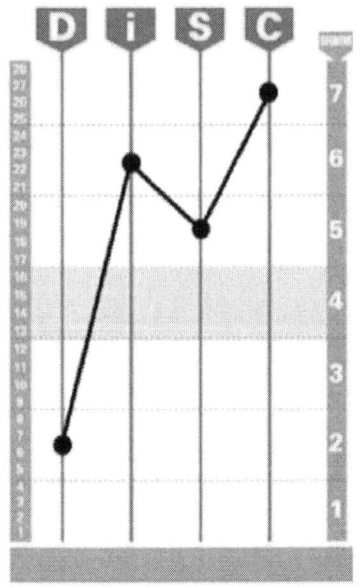

Practitioner

A practitioner is very conscientious but also has high influence and steadiness scores. The dominance score will be very low.

A practitioner enjoys being part of a team and wants everyone to succeed. That person is not comfortable with being a leader but rather, they are a supportive contributor.

Practitioners are willing to take a little longer to come up with ideas. They like environments where people care for each other and know what they want.

The attitudes that a practitioner holds include the following:

- Practitioners are heavily accommodating to others.

- They are motivated by their interactions with others.

- Their skills in the workplace can inspire people.

- Many practitioners like to put their personal goals ahead of others.

- They don't like to take risks often.

A practitioner enjoys doing good things for the team. They tend to be happy and careful in everything they do.

These fifteen attitudes are all measured by the DISC test with the purpose of figuring out how people act. You must review the results of the tests to determine what people in the workplace are like.

You should also be aware of how these people will respond in their working environments. These patterns are caused by the way people react to whatever they see. The next chapter takes a look at the work environment   and how it impacts on people.

Chapter 5 – The Environment

Take a look at the work environment you're in right now. Is it hectic or comfortable? Is it organised or chaotic? Does it seem inviting? Maybe it's in a transitional period and you have no idea what's coming next.

As great as it can be for individuals to work together, there are often problems that come about when we try to get staff members to work in close association, especially for extended periods or during times of stress or change. It is never easy for people to work together, they are unique and different. The changes in an environment are a proof of this.

People will react to their environments in many ways. Some feel more controlled while others aren't so sure. Some are afraid of changes in their working environment.

The DISC test exists to ensure that people can be matched with one another in a logical manner. That is, people who work well with each other in a similar or complementary style.

This helps to maintain a healthy working environment. It also allows all team members to be fully aware of what everyone is doing.

Part of the DISC test entails understanding how people work within their environments. Some people are much more confident about their environments than others.

Every group needs to have people who can keep things in check. The environment must be positive and comfortable to the point where no one will be afraid of what might happen.

The most useful thing about the DISC test is that it focuses on how people **respond.** It's about what people do in a variety of situations.

Some people will be far more aware of office tension or stress than others. Some will experience stress triggers more quickly or easily than others. Every person perceives the environment in a unique way.

Power Over the Environment

The amount of power that someone has over their environment can be a big influence on how they behave. Power can involve control over attitudes as well as tasks in the workplace. These directly influence how people act and react at work.

Power relates to control and keeping yourself from harm. It can even mean getting your way over everyone else.

Most importantly, it relates to how comfortable someone is in the face of change. Those who aren't powerful are often afraid of what will come about. They will try and avoid change as long as possible.

Be aware that power relates to what one can **directly** control. There must be a sense of **direct support for choosing your own path.**

Holding Power

In particular, **dominant and influential people have more power over their environments.** They can get others to follow their ideas.

A dominant person will guide people and tell them what to do. An influential person will encourage or inspire others to follow along with certain ideas.

These people have more power and therefore can do more with their assets. They are **proactive**, they do things in preparation for what could happen.

Also, they are **assertive**, they will do what they can to win. They are adamant about what they want to do.

These people are not always going to try and control others. However, they have the potential to do what they can do get them on the right track.

Lacking Power

Those who are **steady or conscientious will not have much power.** They have little control over their environments.

They are both groups that are comfortable with what's happening. Some of them are just fine with the status quo. Either way, they want to focus on doing, not leading.

They are **adaptive** people who will adjust what they do in accordance with changes. These include changes in rules, environment or the resources open to them.

Those who lack power are also **reactive**; they respond to ideas and concepts. They must find ways to respond or they will be left behind.

Overall, the people who have power tend to be on top of things. They know what to do and aren't afraid of what might happen. They will get along with each other and won't struggle. These people must be in charge of those who are ready to resist change.

Perception of the Environment

The work environment can be perceived in many ways. To some, it can be favourable. That is, a person will feel comfortable. They will not be afraid of what's going on around them and will keep everyone's morale up.

Meanwhile, others will see the environment as being unfavourable. They are willing to question what might be happening.

The favourability of the environment is critical to the success of any employee. Some will accept what's happening and others will try to avoid anything uncomfortable.

Favourable Environment

The people who are **influential and steady will see their environments as friendly and favourable.** They have many great attitudes:

- They are accepting of whatever is going on around them. They hold the heart as being more important than the brain.

- They will agree upon most things in a spot; the potential for debate is extremely unlikely.

- They especially focus on people. This includes being as pleasant as possible.

The favourable environment will entail people being happy about whatever they are doing. They won't feel like they are at risk of harm or danger; they will instead feel ready to take on the world.

Unfavourable Environment

The people who are **dominant or conscientious will see their environment as unfavourable.** They have many unique attitudes:

- They are ready to question anything that comes about.

- They concentrate on logic; heart is not a big point.

- They see everything as a challenge.

- These people aren't willing to side with just anything, they will go against the grain if necessary.

Overall, some people are able to control their environments and will feel motivated to change things. Others will feel a lack of power and try to keep things the same. Either way, these are factors that can directly influence the direction of the team as a whole.

Prepare the Right Number of People

These measurements should be analysed carefully when developing a team. You must be aware of how all four main types of people can act differently in their control and desire for change. Some people will do all they can to impact a group but others will be fine in the background.

You must have at least one person in your group who is capable of keeping things organised. That is, the person **must be able to adjust the environment** to avoid making things needlessly difficult and to ensure the unit functions efficiently and achieves its goals.

Having one person from each major group can also help as it becomes easier for everyone to balance each other out. Still, this does not mean that everything will automatically work out. You must have at least one person who ensures the work environment remains conducive to ensuring that the workforce can actually fulfill its role.

Remember that control over the environment can make a difference when garnering enough people for group activities. There's always that necessity to figure out who has more control over an environment and who sees it in a good light. Make sure you have enough people in each group so you'll hold enough power.

Creating a Conducive Environment for Many

Every type of personality requires its own special environment. People have different demands which can be determined by the way they act. You need to consider how well such the environment is working out for each person. It's all about reducing the stress of having no control over an environment or not feeling supported by it.

Dominant

A dominant personality needs to be in a tough environment. The following features can be found in such an environment:

- The entire environment must be challenging. There must be plenty of opportunities for problem-solving.

- The dominant person needs to have control.

- A sense of leadership and authority is required.

- This person also needs to be involved in a variety of activities. These include activities in different fields. Both short and long-term projects should be covered.

Influential

Influential people want to be appreciated by more people. They often demand the following:

- Influential people want to be recognized. They feel better when they know that others like them and appreciate what they're doing.

- They don't want to deal with lots of details. They prefer things to be simple.

- Influential people don't like being controlled.

- They want to inspire people into doing things. They prefer to focus on the way they can talk with others to make certain ideas sound more appealing or persuasive.

Steady

Steady people prefer some control in their lives. These points are the best ones that they can have in their environments:

- Steady people want their environments to be consistent. They prefer familiarity.

- Steady people also feel best when they're in groups. They want to be surrounded by others who can carry out the tasks that fall outside their own abilities.

- An area of specific functionality is often included. That is, it's a role that people understand and have experience of.

- They want to be supported by others. That is, they want support from others who can do whatever they aren't experienced with. This is so the steady person can focus on what he or she is used to.

Conscientious

Conscientious people like predictability and routine things. These are some of the things they prefer:

- Predictable environments are crucial to a conscientious person. These include places with similar schedules and people.

- The job description must be specific and clear. It must also be consistent.

- Accuracy and care are critical.

- Plenty of planning is also required in the conscientious person's role.

- A conscientious person enjoys challenge and will look for ways to challenge themselves within a stable work environment.

Every type of person has their own attitudes about how their environments should work. It's a necessity to ensure that the best fit of employees are hired for the right jobs.

Stress Triggers in the Environment

Everyone suffers from stress at times. It's a given in any climate. But stress makes it harder for people to get on with their work or feel they are functioning at their best. It especially causes people to rush their work and make mistakes.

Many people will have stress triggers within any kind of environment. There are various ways in which stress can occur in different situations. The following points refer to the most common situations that can crop up in any work environment.

Losing Control

It's easy for people to lose control of their situations. They can lose control because of outside events such as customers getting in the way or even weather-related problems.

Dominant personalities don't like to lose control. They want to stay on top of things. They don't want to be undermined by anything.

Influential people are not going to feel stress because they don't have control. They are perfectly comfortable following orders.

Taking Orders

Orders and commands can create stress for some people. This depends largely on how intense they are or even who is giving the orders. Still, some will feel stressed by commands because they think they are too good to be told what to do. They feel that they should be the ones giving commands.

This is especially the case for dominant personalities. They want to issue orders, not take them. They will feel stressed out if someone tells them what to do.

Steady people will not feel stressed out by orders. They expect to take orders and want to keep their work consistent.

Of course, pretty much anyone can easily feel more stress as a result of an extreme amount of work. Steady people aren't as likely to suffer from stress because of extra work. If anything, they will appreciate being called upon to do so much for others.

A Lack of Progress

There are times when there's no progress in the workplace. It could be from a lack of resources, no real customer demand or even employees not showing up to work or doing what they should be.

A lack of progress can be annoying. It causes work to build up and can create disorganisation in some cases. It can even keep businesses from evolving and taking on newer ideas.

Dominant and influential people are stressed out by this problem. They want to feel they have accomplished something specific and want others to do the same. They won't like it if they can't get their way.

Steady and conscientious people cope better if there isn't much progress. They are more controlled and will just continue to pay attention to commands regardless of whether or not progress is being made. More importantly, the conscientious person will focus on perfection even if it means taking more time to make something right.

A Lack of Appreciation

People want to be appreciated in the workplace. People like it when others acknowledge them and make them feel special. No one wants to be treated like a nameless statistic.

However, in our busy working lives, it can happen. A work environment can be so big that it's tough to keep tabs on everyone. Also, the management or other leadership can be too physically removed from everyone. This often makes it harder for employers to show that they care.

Influential people are stressed out by not having enough appreciation. They want be recognized as people who are highly powerful and controlling. They don't want people to forget about them. They thrive on praise.

Dominant and conscientious personalities won't feel the same stress. They are too busy thinking about the tasks at hand. They feel most comfortable with these tasks when they are fully completed; by then they will focus on what's next and will be less concerned about what people think of them.

Trying to be Perfect

Some people are forced into being as perfect as possible. It's a cutthroat business world; people who aren't perfect can easily be side-lined while the ones that know what they're doing more are pushed forward.

The need to be detailed, controlled and accurate is stressful. Influential people especially struggle with the need to be perfect more than others. They just want people to do their best; they find it harder for them to succeed if they are pressured to do more.

Conscientious people won't feel stressed by this desire. They generally strive to attain perfection. They aren't afraid to focus on details.

Interacting with Others

Interactions come in many forms. Sometimes they entail talking with managers and other groups. In other cases contact is with customers. Either way, speaking is a crucial part of the job.

Steady and conscientious people are often uncomfortable with interactions. They don't like to speak in public and would rather be by themselves. They feel less stress when working on tasks that don't entail interaction.

This is the total opposite for influential people. Influential people enjoy speaking to others and will do anything to interact with people, and would feel stressed in a situation where they had little or no contact with others.

Controlling Stress in the Environment

Every work environment will have its own stresses. These stresses include problems where people are forced to do more work than they can manage comfortably.

Every personality can struggle with stress. This doesn't mean they all have to bear with it for a long time. Every personality can resolve stress-related issues by using a few simple ideas.

This section relates to what people in different DISC positions do to keep stress at bay. They respond to stressful situations in their own ways and aren't afraid of changing things around if it means keeping stress under control. Here's a look at what each group can do in such situations:

Dominant

All dominant personalities think about their overall goals. This includes the long-term picture and how it will be better for everyone. Much of this includes understanding how the final results will look.

Everything that the dominant person does will impact the big picture in some way. They always slow down for a while to think about how they can make things happen.

All of their priorities must be reviewed. These priorities include what's essential for completing tasks and what's merely optional. In the dominant person's mind, the optional priorities can be set aside for later. This is a time to figure out what's more important and crucial to the workplace.

Dominant figures want to do what they can to win. They never forget why they work and keep things in check.

Influential

Influential people do what they can to get people to see things their way. However, they often fail to see that they're just as responsible for causing stress. An influential person will think about their role in the situation and where it's going. This includes an analysis of why things have reached the current stage of events.

The influential person won't focus on how others behave. Rather, they know that other people are doing their hardest to succeed. They are only small pieces in a much larger puzzle.

Influential people will think about the problems that have come around and why they are there. More importantly, they feel accountable for anything that happens. This has the benefit of including the need to figure out what can be done to fix problems.

Steady

Steady people are often okay with taking their time to finish projects. However, sometimes that patience takes its toll.

Patience ensures that things are done as carefully as possible. Still, it also makes the job harder to handle. It causes work to pile up. This only makes the job harder for the steady person plus others are forced into picking up the slack. In addition, the extra work requires more organising.

Steady people must be willing to work faster. They have to be more assertive and active when making decisions.

Steady people should share what they are feeling. They have emotions and ideas relating to their projects; they should be encouraged to share their ideas and feelings with others. In conflict resolution, they should be encouraged to explain how they feel as others can often be unaware of the steady person's feelings.

Conflicts can especially be problematic for steady people; steady people have a tendency to avoid it and resist any desire to consult people with different ideas.

Conscientious

Conscientious people always focus on details. They can adapt to stress by using the data they have to make the right decisions.

These people often adapt by staying positive. They think about their best attributes and go along with them. They aren't afraid to be constructive about themselves.

Most importantly, conscientious people never burrow deep into events to see who's right or right. They want to think more about moving forward and going places. They don't like it when they're stuck in the past.

Bearing with Tension

Tensions can easily rise within the workplace especially over different viewpoints and temperaments. Sometimes the everyday stress of a busy workplace can make matters worse.

The problems that come from tensions can be irritating. However, every person will respond in different ways. People respond in these specific ways:

- Dominant people attempt to use their power to their advantage. They won't think about what others feel. They will take advantage of the situation and wrestle all the power from everyone.

- Influential people will go after others with verbal attacks. They will shift the blame to anyone.

- Steady people will give in to the tension. They will agree with practically anything. They will follow the commands that dominant people issue. They'll also side with an influential person's blame.

- Conscientious people generally try to avoid tension. They aren't willing to be aggressive.

Asking Questions in the Environment

Every person has questions to ask as an environment changes. They want to know many things – why are things changing? What is changing? Who is being impacted by these changes? When are these changes coming? The list goes on.

Every individual responds with different questions. The specific questions to ask vary by each personality:

- Dominant people don't really like to ask questions. They instead just take things as they come. They don't like to have things explained too much.

- Influential people want to explore as many details as possible. There are no limits to what questions they will ask.

- Steady people focus on the "who" and "how" of the situation. They like to know what is going on because they want to figure out what changes are happening and if it affects them.

- Conscientious people focus on the "why" and "what" questions. They need to get details so they'll know what to do in a new situation. They like to feel prepared.

The questions will vary based on the situation of course. Whatever happens, you can expect many workers – or at least those who aren't dominant – to ask lots of questions.

How Feelings Change

Everyone has feelings and ways of sharing them. Some are open to sharing them while others would rather be reserved and private.

Each of the four key types have feelings that can change in many ways. These especially change during stressful situations:

- Dominant people are often frustrated and agitated while under pressure. They don't want to be delayed while stressed. They want to solve their problems as soon as possible.

- Influential people are more emotional than others. They are direct and will share their feelings with anyone. They will especially use them to encourage people to side with them.

- Steady people are willing to share their emotions. They won't do it with just anyone. They focus more on their friends and other peers. They do this with those that they are comfortable with.

- Conscientious people are more controlled. They don't really say all that much to others. Also, they are extremely collected and calculated when they do share their emotions; they don't want to reveal more than necessary.

The ways how these people all adapt to their environments is truly amazing. There's a way for any obstacle to be circumvented and resolved. The DISC test can help find out just what personality one is so it will be easier to figure out who's doing what.

Chapter 6 – Performing the Test

Now that you understand the importance of the DISC test and what its results mean, you can actually perform the test. You must have the right materials on hand first and then a good series of questions.

Contrary to other tests that you've probably taken in the past, the DISC test isn't a make-or-break test. Rather, it's something that can help you and others in the workplace. It gives you an idea of what you or anyone else is like. More importantly, it makes the process of planning new ideas easier to handle.

The questions that are asked are expressive of the attitudes people hold. They must be handled in a professional manner and kept securely. Confidentiality is also paramount.

However, the actual format of the questions can vary. They can be short and easy to use or they can be specific and detailed, requiring more time and effort.

How Questions Work

A DISC test will entail questions that are based on attitudes. These are not direct questions per se; rather, they are attitudes that people have to agree or disagree upon.

A question will consist of a statement; for instance, a person can agree or disagree with saying that he or she is willing to help anyone. Another question might ask about having a positive attitude or whether you think you get your way all the time.

These questions are non-confrontational; they simply ask how people feel about things.

Each question will directly impact the number of points that anyone can score in the test. The points that are used in each question will vary.

These points are tallied up at the end to find a proper score. The higher the score, the more likely someone is to link to a trait.

The total number of questions to use will vary by each test; it is often best to go with at least 50 questions; you could even have twice as many if desired. You need enough to get a more realistic look at your employees.

Also, the test results can be generated by adding up all the points from the answers. In the good old days, this used to be done by hand. Today computers can do it for you while you have a cup of coffee.

The adjustments will have to be made as carefully as possible. You must consider what you want to get out of the scoring process; specifically, you must place even representation among all four attributes when scoring things.

The great thing is, these questions can be about anything. You can add questions relating to specific positions in your organisation, particular behaviours you are looking for and even unique situations such as a particular type of project you know is coming up in the near future. You've got full control over what you want to ask; you just have to think carefully about how these questions will come about.

Two-Answer Questions

Two-answer questions are designed with a simple setup. A person has two choices – yes or no.

Specifically, the choices will relate to a particular statement. A person will have to say if he or she agrees with or disagrees with the statement. This is the easiest type of question to generate.

Here is an example:

1. People tend to look up to me.

    a. Yes   b. No

2. I have a hard time relaxing.

    a. Yes   b. No

3. I am willing to help other people with anything.

    a. Yes   b. No

These three questions should be very easy to answer. The two-answer format is supposed to be very simple.

However, it limits the variance of test results. For instance, a question about dominance can cause one's dominance score to go up by three if a Yes is entered or down by two if a No is used. It does not allow for many other variables.

As you read earlier, this is used in other personality tests more than DISC. The Myers-Briggs test especially uses these questions. While these questions can be good for quick answers, they are not specific or unique enough.

Still, this doesn't mean you can't use them. You can add a large number of them if needed; having several hundred can be useful. You should try to mix in other question styles where you can. More about this later.

Five-Answer Questions

Five-answer questions are a little different. They will use the same kinds of statements but will use five different answers. These are organised based on how someone feels about a statement. Here's an example:

4. I do quite well with motivating other people.

a. Strongly agree   b. Somewhat agree c. Neither agree nor disagree

d. Somewhat disagree   e. Strongly disagree

5. I want to finish things as quickly as possible.

a. Strongly agree   b. Somewhat agree c. Neither agree nor disagree

d. Somewhat disagree   e. Strongly disagree

This allows for more variance in terms of grading. Let's take a look at question 4. An A (strongly agree) would cause the person to get five points on the influence scale. Meanwhile, that total would go to 3 for a B answer, 0 for a C, -3 for a D and -5 for an E.

What this means is that you've got a more accurate way of reviewing what people think. You'll see that some people have more confidence or doubt in specific skills than others. Some don't even know what to think.

Of course, it does take longer to generate questions like these as you will add more point totals. Still, it will give you more detailed results.

A quick note: You can always use something in between the two and five-question format. A three-question format that uses "always," "sometimes" and "never" questions can be used, for instance.

More or Less Questions

A third option for the DISC test is to ask more or less questions. These questions are designed as follows:

1. You will ask the person if something is **more or less** important.

2. This will be followed by a series of answers.

3. The test-taker must choose the answer that one agrees upon. For a **more** question, that person chooses what one puts into more priority. For a **less** question, it goes the other way around.

This format entails figuring out what priorities someone has. Here are a few sample questions:

1. While working, I think that it is **more important** for me to...

   a. Keep the environment under control

   b. Ensure the rules aren't too strict

   c. Know exactly what has to be done and how to do it

   d. Finish jobs and see what happens next

2. If someone says something to me then I will be **less likely** to...

   a. Agree with it

   b. Say something nice in response

   c. Ask for more details

   d. Silently agree and say nothing

You can choose to reverse these questions if you want as well. That is, you can ask a person what they value the most followed by what is valued the least. This leads into the next question format.

Point Value Questions

Point value questions are loosely related to more or less questions. However, every statement must be answered with a point value. Here's how it works:

1. A statement will be made. The test-taker must then review the options.

2. The test-taker will place a point total next to each answer. The value of each point total will vary with each question.

3. The final answer will be a reflection of how important things are to someone.

This is a little more specific as it gives an idea of a person's values.

Here are a few samples:

1. When I am told to do more research on a project, I end up doing it because I (on a scale of 1 to 4, 1 being your least likely response and 4 being your most likely):

a. Enjoy researching

b. Want to get the best results possible

c. Want to make things easier

d. Hope it will get people to respect me

2. If I am at an event with lots of people I have never seen before, I will (on a scale of 1 to 4, 1 being less likely to happen and 4 being most likely)

a. Find anyone I am familiar with and stick with that person

b. Quietly check out the event

c. Talk with whoever I can

d. Focus on very specific people of interest

These questions will give you an idea of what people are thinking. More importantly, it is a measurement of attitudes.

How Totals Are Calculated

The scores that come out of the DISC test will vary based on the answers people give. The values of each question will vary.

A certain answer can cause the score of one attribute to increase while the score of another will go down. This can vary in many ways; for instance, a question about whether or not someone is happy with change can influence one's steadiness ranking. That ranking can go up if that person says he or she is not okay with change.

The two-answer format will allow for an easier time when calculating scores. However, a five-answer format may entail very specific parameters. That is, the rise in one attribute can be greater in intensity if a person answers questions at certain extremes.

You should be cautious when seeing how point totals are issued with certain, ambiguous questions. You'll have to keep everything as even as possible. That is, you need to include two dominance questions followed by two influence questions and so forth. Keep it even for a more accurate review of the general attributes.

Be careful when figuring out what the values for every category are going to be. You should use a maximum of about **30 to 40 points for the highest score and -20 to -30 for the lowest** on each attribute. This range should be strong enough for figuring out who's the strongest and who needs help in certain fields.

A Few Sample Statements

Let's talk for a moment about the questions you'll ask. Your questions must be written in the form of statements. These questions must also be in the first-person.

Here are a few examples:

1. I am in control of my emotions.

2. I tend to obey the rules.

3. I think I am a loyal person.

4. I try to be as accurate as possible in my work.

5. I am kind to others.

6. I like to listen to other peoples' ideas.

7. People like to pay attention to me.

8. No one is bothered by my presence.

9. I am not bothered by anyone's presence.

10. I think before I speak.

We could go on with these statements but those are just a few examples. You'll have to be careful when writing them, as you will see shortly.

Where to Get the Questions

You can find DISC questions in a variety of places. You can always go online to generate a DISC questionnaire, for instance. You can learn about different questions online right now. It would be impossible to list the number of websites that have DISC test papers here.

You can also use a software program or workbook system. These official programs will guide you through the process of generating and administering DISC assessments. Companies like Axiom Software offer many programs to choose from so you'll have more control over your assessments.

Of course, you can always generate questions yourself. But this can take a while and you might want to outsource that work to others.

Be sure to still keep tabs on the quantity of questions. This includes the total number of questions and the attributes that they cover. Try and use an equal number of questions for each individual characteristic.

Preparing the Questions

You must be careful when asking your questions. Make sure you phrase them properly in a variety of ways:

- All questions must be in the first person.

- An active voice should be used at all times.

- Don't just say "always" or "never" if you're using a question with more than two answers.

- You can add a "not sure" option if desired but it's best to leave it out. A "not sure" answer will not adjust one's answers.

- A "not applicable" answer may be used in cases where there's a certain individual situation that not everyone will be involved in.

Feel free to consult any DISC program or expert to figure out what you can do when getting your questions ready. They must be as appropriate and sensible as possible while targeting every attribute you want to highlight.

Avoid Ability-Based Questions

The beauty of the DISC test is that it's not about anyone's ability to do things. It's about how a person feels and thinks. You should not break this point by using ability-based questions.

Ability-based questions refer to how well someone can complete tasks. For instance, you might ask a person to measure one's confidence on whether or not that person is comfortable with operating a particular machine or software program.

These ability-based questions can be very stressful. What's more, some people might alter their responses to those questions just to make themselves look better.

You should not use any of these questions in your test. They will only judge people and make them feel pressured into giving good answers.

Also, these ability-based questions can easily kill off the mood of a test. Your test-taker will not at all happy about the questions. This could cause too much pressure, thus keeping that person from accurately answering all the other questions. You don't want them leaving the test feeling bad about themselves or thinking they are going to lose their job.

Administering the Test

While the test itself can be easy to generate, administering it is another story. You must make sure you keep whoever takes the test comfortable and that they know what to expect.

It's only human nature for people to become worried about tests. We always dreaded those pop tests in school, for instance. However, this shouldn't be treated as a test that can make or break one's future. Rather, it's a test that **explores a person's opportunities.**

You should do the following when actually administering the test:

- Tell the test-taker that there are no wrong answers.

- Assure them that the information will be kept confidential within only a handful of designated people.

- Let people know to be as honest as they can.

- Create an inviting environment for the test to be held in. Don't create a cold or poorly-lit space; make it bright, wide open and relaxing.

- Try not to have anyone else around while the person takes this test. Your presence could be seen as a sign of pressure to answer questions in a certain light.

- Most importantly, don't rush anyone. Make sure whoever answers the questions does so in their own time.

The DISC test is crucial to the development of a business and the creation of a positive and supportive workplace. Taking a test can be tough on people, but don't make it any worse than it has to be. There's always plenty of opportunity in the DISC test. Make sure it's well-constructed and that whoever takes it can actually benefit from it.

Chapter 7 – Reviewing the Results

The DISC test should not be all that hard to facilitate. You can do a whole lot more if you just come up with the right questions and administer the test. But what happens after the test, when you've got lots of results to analyse?

The numbers in the test will be staggering. There are lots of totals and values to calculate; it will be up to you to figure out what everyone scored after the test is done.

The results from the test should be analysed carefully. Your results should be prepared based on the particular answers you get.

The results are generated based on a series of numbers. That is, the positive numbers suggest that a person meets a certain characteristic.

We already looked at a sample readout of how the test

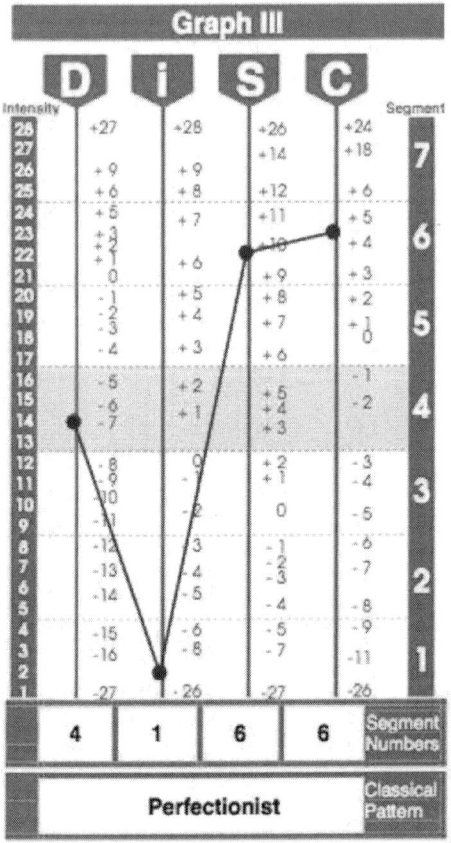

works. This second sample is one that highlights a perfectionist's behaviour.

Notice how this particular edition of the test results has a series of numbers next to each entry. These are reflective of the answers that were given.

You'll have to compare the totals with the patterns that are found here. Many computer programs will highlight the patterns for you automatically.

There are two huge measurements that the test results will feature – the intensity of the answers and the segment that one's profile falls into.

Intensity

The numbering on each attribute is varied. The number is the **intensity.**

The intensity refers to how much or how little one person meets an attribute. Think of it as a measure of extremes – the higher up you are, the more likely you find an attribute.

This number can be positive or negative. This all depends on the number of questions asked.

Also, the way the number is to be organised should depend on the possible maximum or minimum scores. That is, the highest number should be the highest possible score that one could get for an attribute while the minimum is the other way around.

Notice in the chart above how the range of numbers seems to expand over time. That is, the extremes don't come until the very top or bottom range. This means that only those who score in certain extremes should be interpreted as following very specific attributes.

Of course, there is no guarantee that someone will reach either extreme. This just helps to figure out which characteristics one is more likely to meet.

Be sure to watch for how big the intensity can get for each individual attribute. Try and keep the maximum score for each of the four categories as close to one another as possible. You don't want to favour one over all the others or else that will create a test that isn't fully descriptive or explanatory of what makes people tick.

Segment

There are seven sections that the results can be organised through. These sections are known as **segments**.

The segments are ranked from 1 to 7 – 1 being the least likely to show a certain characteristics, 7 being the most likely to show it.

The 4 is shaded; this is the neutral point across society. This is the top of the bell curve were most people sit. You will notice that the average person sits in negative on the D traits, with the norm being -5 to -7, whilst most people exhibit S behaviours, so the norm across society is +3 to +5.

The measurements here are designed to be a guide to how people behave on average. This takes a look at how well people fit in with certain behaviours. A person with a higher segment will have a greater propensity to behave in some way.

Most people will be stuck in the middle segments. However, there's often going to be one segment that people will score higher in. These traits that they exhibit outside of the average are likely to be the ones that most effect how they work and make decisions.

No Right or Wrong Answers

This isn't like any traditional test. There's no such thing as a right or wrong answer here. The test results will simply show you just what skills someone has. Every person will have at least one attribute that scores high.

Think of this as a constructive solution. It focuses more on what you can do. It allows you to build the best team and get the right people in the right roles. It allows you to position people for success by adapting their environment, how they are managed and how they are communicated with to best suit their personal style.

Use a Computer Program or Online Based Test

The process of calculating results can be complicated. You not only have to tally up the answers but also figure out the point values to attach to each individual question. This can be pretty hard to handle.

However, this doesn't have to be too challenging if you have a good computer program, or ideally an online test. Online tests handle the questions, answers and generate a complex report for you.

Most importantly, the online tests will **generate the most accurate reports while saving you time.** This should make the DISC test a little more appealing. If you use the test right, it won't be more complicated than it need be.

Of course, you should only find an online test that you trust, is cost effective and you are able to use. Don't bother with systems that are too confusing, frustrating or complicated.

Ensure your program can share results with others. You could collaborate with others in the workplace over how to make decisions based on test results.

Remember that the results in a DISC test can say a lot about someone. Make sure you understand how you're getting the results ready so you'll have more control over the process.

Chapter 8 – Using the Results

So now you know how to use the DISC analysis to your benefit. It's clearly a popular and useful kind of test. However, you have to think about what you're going to do with the results.

The results will tell you what characteristics a person has and any patterns attached to them. The graphic used to express these results should also be easy to understand.

However, you need to think about how you plan to use your results. You must be cautious when thinking about this.

Fortunately, it's not hard to get the results to work out right for you. You just have to use a few smart ideas.

Consider the Results Carefully

You must analyse the results that you get out of the test as carefully as possible. The results will certainly explain a lot about the people in your workplace and how they operate.

More importantly, you must use a few considerations:

- Which attribute did a person get the best results out of?

- What specific results did the person give for certain questions? This is important if you've got questions that you value over others.

Every single test is taken differently. Watch for how the results come about. They will tell you more about someone than you could have ever imagined.

The pattern that came up should also be reviewed. Sometimes you will find the pattern will be influenced by a few particular questions. Your research can help you find what someone did based on a test.

What Tasks Work Best?

You must observe the tasks that certain people carry out based on the results they get. Take a look at the pattern someone follows and see what jobs suit them best. You will be surprised at what some people can do.

For instance, a persuader could be hired to encourage people to go along with certain ideas. That person could even be in touch with customers to help them see why they should do business with you.

Also, an investigator should be hired for research or inspection purposes. That person is focused on details and will do anything to be accurate and successful.

Think carefully about the tasks that these people will carry out. Always use every single answer to your benefit when figuring out what people could be better at.

Organise Every Group

Depending on the size of your group, you will find a variety of different results. Some will focus on one specific attribute while others lean towards two of them.

Every person in your group is clearly different. With that in mind, you must organise each group as carefully as possible. Take a look at how the people act and try to organise them with other, like-minded people. Make sure they are in groups that they are comfortable with and where they won't struggle.

In fact, you can use a few special considerations for each individual category:

- Dominant people want to be in groups that demand results as soon as possible. They don't want to be stuck in slow situations.

- Influential people are willing to be in practically any kind of group. They just want to share ideas and make people feel excited about what's around.

- Steady people are fine in groups with one another provided that they aren't getting too much attention. They don't want as many responsibilities as dominant people do.

- Conscientious people focus less on variable groups and more on just doing anything. They are willing to stay in groups that aren't going to be rushed.

Any Contradictions?

You should think about the contradictions between the results of a test and the role someone is doing. This is specifically for cases where you are giving the test to someone who's already employed by you.

Sometimes a person will be in a position that focuses on creative thought while that person's responses to the test suggest this is not their strength. This can often explain why a person seems unmotivated. They will likely also be unhappy at this point.

This is typically a sign that something needs to change for a person to stay employed with you. You'll have to send that person to another position or role in the workplace. Try not to terminate that person's employment contract; the DISC test is far from a suitable tool used to determine who should be fired. Rather use the results as a tool to see how you can get the best out of each individual in your team.

Needless to say, every single person in your workforce will respond differently. You can hold follow-up interviews with your test-takers if needed. In fact, that is a part of what the next chapter is about.

Avoid Misusing the System

While the results in the system can be useful and descriptive, that doesn't mean they mean specific things. You must avoid using your DISC results improperly.

Labeling People

Sometimes people are labeled by the results they get in the DISC test. That is, people are suggested as ones that will always do certain things. For instance, you could just assume that a steady person is always going to sit back. You can also think that the influential people are willing to beg for anything.

You must avoid labeling anyone who gets certain results in a test. Labeling isn't good as it makes you look shallow, and you might end up losing a valuable member of staff.

Everyone is able to operate in any quadrant of the DISC traits, it just takes more effort and DISCipline to operate in a quadrant that doesn't come naturally. That takes energy. Whereas operating somewhere you naturally sit allows you to feel more motivated with the task and focus your energy on your role.

Excuses

Sometimes DISC results are used as excuses for why people act like they do. You can see a conscientious person taking forever in a project and then assume that it's because that person is so fixated on details.

In reality, you cannot just judge people based on their DISC results. Rather, you have to think about why people do things and why they act as they do in every situation. Don't ever assume that a conscientious person is taking forever on something just because he or she got that attribute in the test.

Removing People

You can consider letting people go if they have DISC results that you're not fond of. However, that is never a good thing to do.

Removing people from their jobs because of their DISC results is never a good idea. No one wants to lose their job because they didn't get certain scores on their evaluations. Word will get round, and you might have trouble getting people to take a test in future.

Rather, you should move those people to different roles or positions in your workplace. Put them in spots that are conducive to their behaviours. The goal is to make them feel better about the positions they are in. Then they will work harder and better.

Misusing the DISC test is always a dangerous and harmful thing to do. You cannot just adjust your workplace or your attitudes because of how people score. You have to simply adapt the situation around the answers people gave.

You will even want to think about equipping all those people with the right resources. That's where this next section comes into play.

Equipping People

You have to prepare everyone for their roles in the workplace. You must let people take a look at what resources they've got.

The resources in your workplace include everything needed to complete jobs – hardware, software, tools, access to people, skillset, etc.

You must be prepared to help everyone in the workplace with their goals. The specific materials you'll require will vary based on what your business is like.

Either way, you must analyse the behaviours people have and then provide them with the right tools they can use. Anything that they will feel comfortable with is critical; it's all about getting tasks completed.

Commands for Each Attribute

Each DISC profile has its own beliefs on how to respond to commands. You should be cautious when you're giving commands to each one.

Dominant

Dominant people aren't willing to be led by anyone. They prefer to do the leading. That doesn't mean you cannot give commands to a dominant person. You can give commands with a few tips in mind:

- Offer challenging assignments for a dominant person to complete. Dominant people love challenges and exercises that show their power.

- Act like a good model to your workers. Talk about what you do and how you do it. This should help the dominant person to learn more about how to behave properly. This includes understanding how to be a more efficient leader.

- Always place an emphasis on logic.

- Take a look at the possible benefits that will come about in a project.

- Sometimes a dominant person will disagree with you. Ask that person about what he or she wants instead. See if those ideas are relevant to the big picture. If not, see if you have alternatives that you've come up with on your own.

- Be concise, don't go on and on when giving commands. Clear and direct works best for a dominant person.

Influential

Influential people love to be recognized and noticed. It only makes sense that your commands reflect this attitude:

- Give an influential person assignments and projects that allow that person to be visible. These include projects on the sales floor or speaking activities. Anything that enables a person to be noticed is always worthwhile.

- Let the influential person share ideas. Allow a sense of openness but do set some parameters on what's appropriate. You want to let that person come up with great ideas but not be stuck with bad concepts.

- Keep any conversations with an influential person short. That person wants to do the talking, not you.

- Keep the work setting as positive and happy as possible.

- Don't make disagreements worse than needed. Allow time to pass for a bit so the situation can cool down.

Steady

Steady people are often easy to give commands to. They like to listen and aren't willing to ask too many questions. Still, you must know how to give commands right:

- Give out assignments that are very specific. These include tasks that are specific to the skills and goals someone holds.

- Be more personal in your speech. Show that you genuinely care about your worker.

- Give your worker time to feel comfortable around you. Don't ever act rough or harsh on someone. Instead, take time to focus on a positive friendship.

- Focus on some kind of common ground.

- Explain how whatever you want to do will keep things as balanced and calm as possible. That is, talk about how something won't change too much.

Conscientious

Conscientious people will also listen to you but they are inquisitive. They want to know why you want to talk with them.

- Explain in detail everything that you want done. Be specific about things like why you want certain tasks completed and how things are to be done. Be technical if you have to.

- Give your conscientious employee time to think about the best way to carry out a task. Don't ever rush any decisions.

- Any tasks that are to be given should be ones that focus on accuracy. These include tasks that involve extremely detailed ideas and a need to be exact.

- Talk openly about how things are done. Share a conversation over how routines work and what can be done to improve certain processes.

Naturally, you are expected to adapt to all the needs that these people have. That's the sign of an effective leader.

Remember that everyone has their own ideas on how to behave. Your organisational plans must be designed based on how well people can respond to different situations and how they score on the test.

Chapter 9 – Resolving the Drawbacks

Like with any other test, the DISC assessment has its own series of drawbacks. Remember, nothing is ever perfect.

Some people have issues with how the DISC assessment doesn't go deep enough into particular situations. Others feel that it is hard to validate the test, what with the fact that so many things can go into the test-taking process.

Still, you don't have to let these drawbacks get in the way of a good team-based project. There are a few ways you can take care of the problems that the DISC assessment can bring about.

Understanding Motives

There are often times when people struggle to take the DISC test. These include times when a person feels too much stress or pressure. This problem can cause a test-taker to rush through the test. Some can even fill out certain answers out of fear. While the test has no wrong answers, some will not believe this.

You can confirm some of these answers by **completing interviews with test-takers.** You can talk with your subjects about their answers. Ask them why they feel as they do about themselves. You can uncover some real feelings.

You may even find that some people have attitudes that are different because they just want to look good. Remember, there's no shame in asking people why they think as they do. You need to do more than learn about your workers or candidates. You need to help them learn more about themselves so they can become better people.

This is great but you must be cautious. **Don't ever explicitly talk about the test with any interviewee.** You must keep them from thinking that you spied on their test results. You need to keep your interviewees comfortable so they will give you accurate answers and feedback.

The Emotional Quotient

Everyone has emotions; some are stronger than others. The worst part is that some emotions can influence one's feelings in a particular situation.

Some people have outside factors that influence their emotions. From struggles in the family to financial problems, these outside problems can cause tension or stress.

In other cases these emotions may be influenced by the brain. Mental disorders like depression or bipolar disorder can cause the brain to function improperly. This will cause a person to suffer from emotional issues that can cloud their normal functions.

These outside factors can cause anyone to answer questions in an unusual manner. Their judgments will be clouded because they have nothing else to think about.

You need to be cautious when giving exams like the DISC test to people with emotional concerns. You can do a few things to prepare someone:

- Create a relaxing environment for the test.

- See if a person who has a mental condition is getting the appropriate treatment for it.

- Allow a person to relax for a few minutes before the test begins. This should be near the environment for the actual test.

These are simple ideas but they can make a world of difference. Being emotionally relaxed means having a clear mind and performing well.

Validation Problems

The DISC test takes a look at how someone responds to problems. It doesn't necessarily test how proficient that person can be.

You can validate the results of a test by using **simulated exercises or tests**. These include tests relating to one's potential position. In addition, you can always administer a follow-up test that asks how they would respond to certain situations.

This should help you see how someone will respond to activities in the workplace. It can confirm any DISC test result.

This is ideal for existing employees. You can always test them to see if they would work better in different positions or if they're best to stay where they already are.

A Lack of Details in the Test

The details used within the test can be limited at times. Sometimes tests have questions with too few answers.

You can choose one of two things to fix this problem. First, you can **add questions with more answers or questions with rank-based answers.** This can add more detail to the test.

Second, you can **use more questions in total.**
Going as deep into someone's mind as possible is
always the best thing to do. It lets you figure out who's
right and who's wrong.

Tough to Review Answers on Their Own

One big problem comes from how the answers
manifest themselves. Sometimes you will pass up the
best available candidate for a position in favour of a
bad one. This is all because you relied too heavily or
too specifically on the DISC results. Or it was the only
technique you used for interviewing a potential
employee

You should **schedule a follow-up interview with
every test-taker**. You can use this time to ask
questions about each person.

The questions must help to clarify or confirm the
results of the test. Ask questions on how they would
respond to certain situations. See how comfortable that
person is with them. Most importantly, see if that
person really shows some interest.

This should help you see if the results in a test are
consistent with someone's attitudes. You don't want to
hire someone based on DISC results only to find that
person is not as proficient as you thought.

These drawbacks to the DISC test may seem substantial but you shouldn't think of them as obstacles. Rather, they are opportunities guaranteed to help you figure out what you can do to make the test more effective and ideal.

Chapter 10 – What If You Take It?

You're read quite a bit about how the DISC test works and how you can create it. But what if you were to take it yourself?

This chapter explains what should be done when administering the test. While it will give you ideas on how to take care of test-takers, they also tell you what you should experience when taking it yourself.

The problem with tests is that people often feel pressured. Think about your schooldays when your teachers administered tests. Did you feel anxious? Did the environment around you feel uncomfortable?

You must be cautious when setting the atmosphere that a test will be taken in. You cannot just let people take it anywhere. You have to establish a comfortable and pleasant atmosphere that has no judgments or negativity. This is to keep people from having a tough time completing it.

However, there are many more things that you have to take a careful look at. You must be certain when taking the DISC test that you get an idea of what you want to get out of the test.

You can use this to help other test-takers feel comfortable with the process. This is to keep them from giving you false responses or from feeling pressured. Of course, you should use these points yourself if you ever have to take a DISC test.

Take Plenty of Time

Anyone completing the DISC test must have time to actually go through it at a comfortable pace. The questions can contain lots of complicated rules or words. You must let yourself or whoever takes it spend enough time on the test.

Remember that this is an untimed test. It is best to allow **30 to 60 minutes** to complete the test on average. This should give anyone time to carefully read the questions and give the best results.

You can always give more time to anyone if the test is really long. Don't place any timers or clocks in the test-taking area either. Remember that everyone will respond to the test in their own ways.

Do it All at Once

The test questions are complicated enough as they are. Do not create breaks during the test or it will become even more complicated.

The types of questions that are asked can vary. These include two, three and five-answer questions plus ones that require ordering options, as listed earlier here. People who do the entire test at once will be less likely to lose track. You'll end up struggling to stick with the proper testing process if you take a break.

Besides, the test isn't going to take long. You just have to answer the questions carefully.

Think About Instincts

Sometimes your instinct can be the key to an answer. That is, a test-taker must stick with one's gut feeling.

It's not always easy to go with one's gut feeling. However, it can be best if you aren't sure what to answer. Remember, **there is no such thing as a wrong answer here. You can stick with your gut feeling.**

The purpose for this is to let the test-taker move forward from one question to the next. People who spend too much time with one or two questions will struggle after a while. This leads into the next point.

Whether it's you or someone else, make sure the proper instincts are followed. Let people answer the questions in a calm and orderly manner.

Avoid Over-Analysis

It's far too easy for people to over-analyse questions. They will think there are extreme specifics and rules in a question that haven't been revealed. They will ask more questions about them than necessary, thus making the test harder.

Some questions will not be sensible but that's not the point. Relating to the last point, you have to use your gut instinct with some questions. That means not analysing questions to the point where you question their existence.

You should not over-analyse things when taking a test. You should impart this to anyone else who takes it. Let them know that they're not going to be judged on whatever they answer. Rather, let them answer the questions themselves without thinking too deeply into the process.

Avoid Distractions

There are plenty of distractions in life these days. From cellphones to sound-systems, there are many problems that can come about.

Always avoid distractions when taking the DISC test. Many things can be done:

- Turn off all cellphones or other devices.

- Don't think about other people in the room.

- Focus on each question and think carefully.

- Don't bring any foods or drinks into the testing area.

- Try and keep any clocks from being visible; the DISC test should be untimed.

You should use these rules when administering the test to others. Don't let anyone feel distracted or bothered by other things going on. Your test-takers will finish the test on time if you keep distractions at bay.

More importantly, they won't feel worried. They won't think about time passing or other forces that can influence their performance.

Chapter 11 – Frequently Asked Questions

Everyone has their own series of questions to ask with regards to using the DISC test. Here's a look at some of the most common questions that crop up.

Do you need to be certified in any way to administer this test?

You don't have to be certified in any manner to actually give out the test. All you need is a program or mindset devoted to creating a test.

Is there a potential for someone's DISC profile to change over time?

Like with anything else in life, there's always going to be that potential for attitudes and behaviours to change. Therefore, you should probably administer this test to people every few years. Sometimes you will find cases where a person isn't as motivated as they used to be.

Can you fire someone because of the results that came from the test?

You technically could but that doesn't mean you should. Firing a person because of one's DISC test results is not the best thing to do. It could be an unjustified means of letting someone go. You could leave yourself open to a wrongful dismissal suit.

Is there a type of style suggesting that people can adapt to use multiple strengths? That is, can someone go from one strength to the next on a whim?

While people can have a blend of different skills, most people will veer towards one above all else. Therefore, there's no way a style like this can exist.

Are the answers in the DISC test definite predictions of how someone can act?

This test just takes a look at what behavioural traits someone has. It focuses on what someone has a propensity for doing. That doesn't mean that person will be guaranteed to act in a certain way.

Can you get a trainer to help you out?

You can always hire a trainer to give you ideas on how to handle the creation of a test. You must make sure the testing process is generated properly so it's not harder to handle than needed. Also, a trainer should be selected based on one's experience with the program, the resources one has and so forth.

Can you get your test results reviewed based on how many people in one group are involved?

You could get group results if desired. You'd have to gather a series of individual results and combine them through a software program. You can use this to generate a composite of the combined results of a grouping of people.

This could give you ideas on which people work best together or how individuals might form a perfectly neutral group if generated right. However, you must be cautious when using a software program for this purpose. It may not generate the best combined results. It might also favour certain characteristics more than others.

Is it a good idea to hide a DISC report from an employee?

You could try and hide the report if desired. This is unlikely to get you the best result.

If you let each employee know their DISC style, the style of the others in the team and, most importantly, your style, they will be better equipped to communicate successfully with everyone. If you are a high D, an S or C may annoy you in how long they take to make decisions or present overly thorough information. Once they can see how your style likes information delivered, they can strive to communicate to you in that way.

You could choose to share these results with an employee before a training session begins too. This is completely optional though.

Can this test be used at any time?

It certainly can work whenever you want. You can even take care of this on an annual or biennial basis if desired.

Is there a potential for emotions to get in the way of a test?

The problem with some people is that they might have emotions over their jobs, their lives and or anything else. These emotions might cloud their judgment while taking the test. This is a drawback that can get in the way unless you get your test-taker to relax and be calm before taking the test.

Conclusion

The DISC analysis has truly been a popular tool for use among many businesses. It has been used for decades to figure out how people behave. This includes a review of the behavioural traits that people have.

It's become more popular in recent times thanks to its efficiency and usefulness. However, it's far from new. In fact, the concept of analysing people based on their attitudes over their skills has been around for close to a century. It was designed to give a realistic idea of how people behave and act.

This test has been around in some form at least 1928. Famed psychologist William Moulton Marston created this theory back then. And for those who are wondering, yes, this is the guy who created the famous Wonder Woman comic book character. He thought that comic books could educate people.

However, throughout his career, Marston focused on understanding how people learn and act. He felt that there was a strong connection between attitudes and proficiency. He especially felt that it was love, not force, that could be more powerful than anything else. In fact, this concept was the basis for the Wonder Woman character.

The biggest development that Marston found was that the behaviours of people are based on two measurements. First, there's the attention that people enjoy. Some are passive while others are active. In particular, dominant and influential people are active while steady and conscientious people are passive.

Second, he felt that an individual's view of their surroundings was crucial. People found them to be favourable or unfavourable. Influential and steady people are comfortable with their environments. The same cannot be said for dominant or conscientious people.

He felt that the need to generate accurate readouts of what people think was important. In fact, he was involved in many early polygraph tests. He wanted to create a new way of seeing how people behave by basing it on the attitudes people hold and how they act.

This form of analysis was unique. However, it was not originally designed to determine behaviours. This led to another evolution in 1956.

In 1956, psychologist Walter Clarke adjusted Marston's findings to adapt the DISC concept into a unique test. This came in the form of the Activity Vector Analysis.

The analysis required people to answer questions based on their attributes. People would state if they related to certain adjectives. It was designed for business-use to help organisations figure out who should be hired.

Over time, many organisations have updated or adjusted the DISC assessment test. From the creation of new answer-formats to the establishment of unique grading schedules, the DISC test has truly evolved.

Today the DISC test has become a standard for analytical purposes. You'd be amazed at the extensive variety of firms that offer DISC training. The number of companies that offer DISC-related software has expanded in size too.

So, what are you going to use the DISC test for? Well, it can work when you're trying to figure out what direction you want your business to go in.

Just think of the many ways you can use this test to your benefit:

- The test can help you figure out which employees are best to hire in your workplace.

- It also helps you see who should be promoted.

- You'll see why people act like they do based on their test results.

- You can learn about what job skills someone can offer.

- You can even use it to determine who has changed over time. That is, you can see if someone's results have evolved in some way.

It's all done to give you a better idea of who's doing what in the workplace. You must use the DISC assessment if you want to succeed.

Remember, the people in your workplace can mean more to you. These people will influence how productive your business is and whether or not customers will support it. You must have the best possible idea of what you're going to get out of the people you hire.

Most importantly, you need to see that you're using your test results right. You can always review the results based on how questions were answered and what patterns emerge. This will help you make decisions on things like what job someone should be in or how to assign tasks. You'll even learn how to interact with someone.

Remember, your employees are more than just skilled workers. They are also people with emotions and feelings. They need to be taken seriously at all times. The DISC test makes it easier for you to do that.

The DISC test will give you the knowledge you need in a secure and comfortable manner. Instead of asking about how people do certain tasks, you'll ask how people feel about their work and their motives. You'll understand a little more about your workers through what they do and why they do it. This in turn will give you that extra bit of control over your workplace.

The DISC test will certainly work wonders for you. Be sure to plan your edition of this test now. Besides, this test is so impressive and efficient that your competition is probably using it too.

An accomplished entrepreneur and speaker, Craig D Robinson has started, grown and exited 3 companies across different industries before retiring at age 34.

Craig first used DISC when faced with the need to grow his team from 25 to over 70 staff in under 3 months. DISC allowed him to recruit the right people into the right roles with minimal disruption and fewer mis-hires.

Craig is passionate about wellness and adventure. He has completed several trail ultra-marathons, is a qualified skydiving instructor and an avid adventure racer. He stays focused and balanced by spending 7 days in silent meditation every 2 months.

A Father, volunteer firefighter, philanthropist and owner of multiple businesses, Craig also finds time to volunteer with children who suffer from disability and children who have been orphaned through parental drug use.

Craig also consults with a wide range of companies, specialising in creating and implementing systems to outsource mission critical roles.

To connect with Craig, visit www.craigdrobinson.com

Printed in Great
Britain
by Amazon

31551637R00111